BIBLE STU

OLD TESTAMENT

THE DALLAS HIGH SCHOOLS
SEPTEMBER, 1954

BULLETIN No. 150
AUTHORIZED BY THE BOARD OF EDUCATION
SEPTEMBER 14, 1954

DALLAS INDEPENDENT SCHOOL DISTRICT
DALLAS, TEXAS

8M—4978—54

BOARD OF EDUCATION

———

EDWIN L. RIPPY, M.D., *President*

MRS. TRACY H. RUTHERFORD, *Vice-President*

JACK H. BREARD   MRS. VERNON D. INGRAM

FRANKLIN E. SPAFFORD   R. L. DILLARD, JR.

ROUSE HOWELL   VAN M. LAMM

———

ADMINISTRATIVE OFFICERS
DALLAS INDEPENDENT SCHOOL DISTRICT

———

W. T. WHITE
Superintendent of Schools

FRANK L. WILLIAMS
Assistant Superintendent in Charge of Instruction

EWELL D. WALKER
Assistant Superintendent in Charge of Personnel

ROBERT H. McKAY
Assistant Superintendent in Charge of Administration

BRYAN ADAMS
Secretary - Business Manager

DON E. MATTHEWS
Assistant to the Superintendent

FOREWORD

The plan for accrediting Bible study in the Dallas high schools for work done out of school is an outgrowth of a movement begun in Dallas twenty-seven years ago by the "Volunteer Bible Study Association for High School Credit." Shortly after this plan was inaugurated, need was felt for a syllabus or outline that would supply materials more suitable for local conditions than those found in any available textbook. The first local syllabus, *Bible Study Exercises*, was printed in 1927. Through the cooperation of teachers of the Bible credit classes and of the pastors interested in the Bible credit work, a much fuller course—the *Bible Study Course*—was published in 1928, reprinted in 1929, and revised and reprinted in 1931, 1935, and 1939.

In 1940 it was decided to offer two separate Bible credit courses, one on the Old Testament and another on the New Testament. The present courses were published in 1946.

The Old Testament course is intended to give a general knowledge of the Old Testament and to present a study of topics that will be of vital interest and importance to students of high-school age. Attempt has been made to avoid controversial questions by emphasizing the study of the Bible itself, thus leaving teachers and pupils free to put their own interpretations on the passages studied. Sufficient flexibility is allowed to permit introduction of other topics than those designated. The standards of work and the procedures followed are expected to approximate as closely as possible those used in the day school.

Grateful acknowledgment is made to all those who have helped, through suggestions or committee service, in the preparation of the present course of study and of the earlier Bible study courses.

W. T. WHITE,
Superintendent of Schools

The Bible is a book in comparison with which all others, in my eyes, are of minor importance, and which in all my perplexities and distresses has never failed to give me light and strength.

ROBERT E. LEE.

Reprinted in 1994 by WallBuilders

For additional copies of this book, for information on other books, or to arrange presentations of this material to groups, contact WallBuilders, P.O. Box 397, Aledo, Texas, 76008, (817) 441-6044.

Published by:

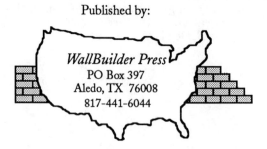

WallBuilder Press
PO Box 397
Aledo, TX 76008
817-441-6044

Printed in the United States of America

ISBN 0-925279-44-7

CONTENTS

	Page
FOREWORD	iii
REGULATIONS GOVERNING THE COURSE	ix

INTRODUCTION —

Minimum Requirements	x
Suggestions to Teachers	xii
Suggested Time Allotment of Lesson Topics	xiv

BIBLE STUDY COURSE: OLD TESTAMENT

INTRODUCTORY LESSON	3

I. *Early Period* —

Introduction	6

Lesson Topics:

1. The Creation	6
2. The Temptation	7
3. Cain, Abel, and Enoch	8
4. The Flood	8
5. The origin of the Races, the Tower of Babel, and Confusion of Tongues	9

II. *Patriarchal Period* —

Introduction	10

Lesson Topics:

6. Abraham and Lot	10
7. Abraham and His Sons	10
8. Jacob and Esau	11
9. Jacob, Rachel, and Laban	11
10. Joseph and His Troubles	12
11. Joseph and His Success	12
12. The Book of Job	13
Map — Ancient Bible World	14

CONTENTS—*Continued*

Page

III. *Early National Period*—

Introduction 16

Lesson Topics:

    13. Moses 16

    14. The Plagues 17

    15. The Exodus 17

    16. Wilderness Experiences 18

    17. The Tabernacle 20

        Plan of the Tabernacle 22

        Camp of Israel 23

    18. The Conquest and Settlement of Canaan . 24

    19. The Time of the Judges 24

    20. Samuel, the Last of the Judges 25

        Map—The Journey from Egypt to Canaan 26

        Fifteen Judges of Israel 27

        Map—The Twelve Tribes of Israel . . . 28

    21. Ruth 29

IV. *Monarchic Period*—

Introduction 29

Lesson Topics:

    22. The United Kingdom—Saul 30

    23. The United Kingdom—David 31

    24. The United Kingdom—Solomon 31

    25. The Temple 32

        Ground Plan of the Temple 34

    26. The Psalms 35

    27. Proverbs, Ecclesiastes, and Song of
        Solomon 36

CONTENTS—*Continued*

		Page
28.	The Divided Kingdom—Israel	38
29.	The Divided Kingdom—Israel (Concluded)	39
30.	The Divided Kingdom—Judah	39
31.	The Divided Kingdom—Judah (Concluded)	40

V. *The Period of Foreign Rule—*

Introduction 41

Lesson Topics:

32.	Judah's Exile	41
33.	Judah's Return from Exile	43
34.	Judah's Return from Exile (Concluded)	44
35.	Esther	45
36.	Prophets	46
37.	Prophecies Concerning the Coming of Christ	48
	Chart of the Most Prominent Old Testament Prophets	49
	Map—New Testament Palestine	52
38.	John the Baptist, the Forerunner of Christ	53
39.	Review Lesson	54

APPENDIX—

Selected Bibliography	57
The Land and the Book—*Wiggins*	59
Important Peoples of Bible Times	63
Language and Manuscripts of the Bible—*Sneed*	65
Literary Characteristics of the Bible—*Lee*	67
Bible History, a History of Redemption—*Dalton*	70
The Old Testament Canon	73
Classification of the Books of the Bible	74
Required Memory Passages	75
Specimen Examination Questions	79

THE GLOSSARY 87

I consider an intimate knowledge of the Bible an indispensable qualification of a well-educated man. Contact with the finest influences which have ever come into human life can be obtained only in this way.

ROBERT A. MILLIKAN.

REGULATIONS GOVERNING THE COURSE

1. Classes may be organized by any Sunday school or church or any other religious organization for the purpose of studying the Bible in their respective organizations with a view to obtaining high-school credit. Successful completion of the course gives one-half unit of credit toward high-school graduation.

2. An application blank, giving necessary information about the class, must be filled out and filed with the Assistant Superintendent in Charge of Instruction of the Dallas Independent School District.

3. There must be a minimum of forty class periods of 90 minutes net teaching time; or sixty 60-minute periods, net time; or eighty 45-minute periods, net time. *In no case will fewer than forty different class periods be accepted.*

4. The text used must be the *Bible Study Course, Old Testament*, prepared for the Dallas High Schools. Supplementary materials may be used at the discretion of the teacher.

5. The teacher must have a minimum preparation of at least a high-school education, and sufficient teaching experience or training in Bible to warrant success in teaching a Bible course. Graduation from college is desirable.

6. There must be a suitable room in which to conduct the class work. A small library of reference and supplementary books is highly desirable and necessary for the best work.

7. Accurate record of attendance and date of class meetings must be kept.

8. This course is open to high school pupils of the ninth, tenth, and eleventh grades and should be completed by seniors or twelfth grade pupils one-half year before graduation.

9. All pupils who desire credit must pass an examination held under the auspices of the Board of Education. This examination will be at the close of the school year or at some other approved time. Final examination questions will be based on the Bible Study Course, and will be confined largely to the items included in "Minimum Requirements" of this course. Pupils who fail on the examination will not be given a second test but will be required to repeat the course in order to secure credit. A deferred examination may be given pupils who are unavoidably prevented from taking the regular examination.

10. Before a pupil is eligible to take an examination for credit in Bible, certification of his having fulfilled the necessary requirements must be made by his Sunday school superintendent and teacher. Forms for this purpose are supplied by the Assistant Superintendent in Charge of Instruction, Dallas Independent School District.

INTRODUCTION

MINIMUM REQUIREMENTS

This course is in itself a "minimum course," since teachers are expected to supplement rather than take from the topics included. For the purpose of emphasis and review, however, a summary of requirements as to what should be expected of pupils follows:

1. Ability to name and classify the books of the Bible.

2. Knowledge of general facts about the Bible, and ability to give a brief history of the Bible under the periods or divisions given in the text.

3. Recognition of and familiarity with the best known short stories of the Bible. The following selected list is taken from Stevens's *The English Bible*, Chapter XXI, page 169:

    a. Joseph. Gen. 37-48.
    b. Balaam and Balak. Num. 22-24 (optional).
    c. The capture of Jericho. Jos. 6.
    d. The wars of Gideon. Judg. 6-8.
    e. Jephthah's daughter. Judg. 11.
    f. Samson. Judg. 14-16.
    g. Ruth. The entire book.
    h. David and Goliath. I Sam. 17.
    i. David and Jonathan. I Sam. 18-20.
    j. Elijah and Phophets of Baal. I Kings 18.
    k. Naboth's vineyard. I Kings 21.
    l. The ascension of Elijah. II Kings 2.
    m. Esther. The entire book.
    n. The three Hebrew children. Dan. 3.
    o. Daniel in the lions' den. Dan. 6.
    p. Jonah. The entire book.

4. Ability to reproduce from memory the following:

    a. The names and the classifications of the books of the Old and New Testaments (See page 74).
    b. The names of the Tribes of Israel.
    c. Genesis 1:1.
    d. Gen. 3:12.
    e. Gen. 3:19.
    f. Gen. 4:9.
    g. Gen. 4:10.
    h. Numbers 6:24-26.
    i. The Ten Commandments, Exodus 20:1-21.
    j. I Samuel 3:10.
    k. Psalm 1.
    l. Psalm 19:14.
    m. Psalm 23.
    n. Psalm 91:1-2, 11.
    o. Proverbs 3:5-6.
    p. Ecclesiastes 12:1.
    q. Ecclesiastes 12:13.
    r. Micah 6:8.
    s. The Great Commandment, Matthew 22:37-40.
    t. II Timothy 2:15.
    u. II Timothy 3:16.
    v. II Peter 1:21.

Note: These memory passages are printed in full on pp. 75-79.

5. Ability to identify all quotations given.

6. Ability to give the meaning of the following terms:
Bible, gospel, Pentateuch, patriarch, "promised land," monotheism, polytheism, theocracy, altar, tabernacle, temple, synagogue, miracle, parable, gentile, covenant, prophecy.

7. Familiarity with the following Bible characters: Adam,
Eve, Cain, Abel, Enoch, Noah, Abram (Abraham), Isaac,
Jacob (Israel), Joseph, Moses, Aaron, Joshua, Samson, Sam-
uel, David, Jonathan, Solomon, Esther, Naomi, Ruth, Isaiah,
Elijah, Elisha, Jeremiah, Nehemiah, Ezra, Job, Jonah, Daniel,
Jesus, John the Baptist, Mary, Elizabeth.

8. The making of the following maps:

a. Abraham's original home and the migrations.
b. Egypt and the Exodus. See p. 26.
c. Palestine in the time of Christ. See p. 52.

9. Familiarity with the following geographical features:

a. *Places*—Ur, Haran, Nineveh, Babylon, Kadesh-Barnea, Shechem, Hebron, Bethel, Jerusalem, Jericho, Bethlehem, Tyre,
Damascus.
b. *Countries*—Chaldea, Babylon, Egypt, Goshen, Peninsula of
Sinai, Galilee, Samaria, Judea, Phoenicia, Syria.
c. *Rivers*—Tigris, Euphrates, Nile, Jordan.
d. *Seas*—Persian Gulf, Mediterranean Sea, Red Sea, Dead Sea.
e. *Mountains*—Mt. Ararat, Mt. Sinai, Mt. Hor, Mt. Nebo, Mt.
Moria, Mt. Gilboa, Mt. Hermon, Mt. Carmel, Lebanon
Mountains.

10. Ability to use concordance and Bible maps.

11. Regular attendance upon the meetings of the class. All
absences should be made up by special meetings or examination over the work missed, as in the day school. Excessive
absence will result in failure to receive credit.

12. Fair knowledge of the lessons studied, and ability to
make a minimum grade of 70 on the final examination. Pupils
should be able to answer such questions as those given in connection with the lesson topics, and in "Specimen Examination
Questions," pages 79-85.

*Try to comprehend as much as possible of this
book with your mind, and accept the rest on faith,
and you will live and die a better man.*
ABRAHAM LINCOLN.

SUGGESTIONS TO TEACHERS

The following brief suggestions are offered for the help of teachers:

1. Members of the class should be impressed at the outset with the value of a knowledge of the Bible, both from a cultural and a personal point of view. They should be further impressed with the fact that this course demands definite standards and attainments, and that it must be studied with the same care and preparation as is required in day-school courses. During the course the teacher will make clear to the pupil the influence of the Bible on the development of English literature, and call attention to the variety of literary forms found in the Bible—narratives, short story, proverbs, poetry, songs, drama, love stories, etc. The newly inserted "Introductory Lesson" should help give pupils a right outlook on the course.

2. In order to avoid possible misunderstandings and confusion, it is necessary that careful attention be given at the outset by teacher and students to the regulations governing credit for Bible work, found on page ix of this book.

3. As a rule, the topics should be studied in the order in which they are listed. Supplementary topics and review lessons may be added at the discretion of the teacher. Sufficient details should be given in connection with each lesson studied to make the meaning clear.

4. The amount of time to be devoted to the different topics is left to the discretion of the teacher. See page xiv for suggested time allotment.

5. The teacher should make sure that the pupils understand clearly the assignments—that they know exactly what is expected of them for each lesson. Items that are not likely to be remembered in connection with the assignments should be written in a notebook or special assignment book.

6. Pupils should be required to keep systematically some kind of notebook, containing special assignments, questions for study, special readings and outlines, quotations and memory passages, special maps, and such other items or notes as the teacher may think best to give.

7. Due consideration should be given to the geography of the countries studied and to the manners and customs of the times. At appropriate times pupils should be asked to read the geographic materials in the Appendix to this course and consult other available books which contain fuller information of this kind.

8. Systematic attention should be given to the quotations and memory passages listed in connection with each lesson presented, and to such other choice passages as the teacher and pupils may select. Required memory passages are indicated under "Minimum Requirements," page x, and for convenience of review these are quoted on page 75.

Pupils are not required to memorize the quotations given in connection with the lesson topics, but they should become familiar with these and be able to identify them or explain their meaning on a test. See footnote, page 7.

9. A portion of each class period may profitably be devoted to oral and written tests. Occasionally full-period reviews and written tests should be given, as in the day school. Pupils may be asked to bring original questions, conduct memory tests, spelling matches, and make-believe radio contests.

10. Special report cards for certifying to parents, from time to time, the character of Bible work being done will be supplied teachers who wish to use them. These cards are intended for the information of parents and for stimulating interest in the Bible work, and are not in any case to be taken as official school records.

11. For several years teachers of the Bible credit classes have maintained an effective organization which meets at regular intervals during the school year. Apart from the fellowship and inspirational features, these meetings have proved very helpful in giving teachers a common understanding of the problems involved in teaching the Bible course and have done much to unify the work. Attendance upon these meetings is entirely voluntary; but teachers can hardly afford to miss them, especially teachers who are giving the Bible course for the first time.

12. In order to do the most effective work, both teacher and pupil should possess needed supplementary materials and aids. A suggested list of helpful books is given on pages 57-58. Usually the church or Sunday school will be willing to supply a reasonable amount of supplementary helps, including wall maps.

————

A man has deprived himself of the best there is in the world who has deprived himself of intimate knowledge of the Bible.

WOODROW WILSON.

SUGGESTED TIME ALLOTMENT OF LESSON TOPICS

Lesson periods may be of varying lengths—90, 60, or 45 minutes; but the 90-minute period has, on the whole, proved the most satisfactory. Under this plan the class is usually conducted from 9:30 to 11:00 on Sunday mornings. Under no arrangement can fewer than 40 regular class sessions be held to meet requirements. (See page ix.) The teaching time devoted to particular lesson topics is optional and will vary with different situations. The suggestions which follow are based on the experience of teachers who have taught the course over a period of years:

1. Introductory—1 lesson

   a. Importance of the Bible: What great men think of it, its relation to history and to literature; cultural and personal values.

   b. Brief historical sketch of the Bible period; general information about the books of the Bible. Exact order and classification of books to be learned as class proceeds.

   NOTE: "Introductory Lesson" has recently been added. See p. 13.

2. Early Period—5 lessons
3. Patriarchal Period—7 lessons
4. Early National Period—9 lessons
5. Monarchic Period—10 lessons.
6. Period of Foreign Rule—6 lessons.
7. Review Lesson—1 lesson

The above suggested allotment is based on 90-minute lesson periods. Teachers who use 60-minute periods or 80-minute periods will plan to have 60 to 80 class periods and will consequently have to divide some of the lesson topics from time to time. Under either the 60-minute or the 80-minute plan it will be necessary to hold extra class meetings on some work day or on Sunday afternoons.

Much of the review work should be done in connection with the lesson topics and at the close of the different periods studied. This same procedure will also apply to literary characteristics of the Bible. In this connection the teacher should read pages 67-70 of this book.

BIBLE STUDY COURSE
OLD TESTAMENT

THE BIBLE

Born in the East and clothed in Oriental form and imagery, the Bible walks the ways of all the world with familiar feet and enters land after land to find its own everywhere. It has learned to speak in hundreds of languages to the hearts of men. It comes into the palace to tell the monarch that he is a servant of the Most High, and into the cottage to assure the peasant that he is a son of God. Children listen to its stories with wonder and delight, and wise men ponder them as parables of life. It has a word of peace for the time of peril, a word of comfort for the time of calamity, a word of light for the hour of darkness. Its oracles are repeated in the assembly of the people, and its counsels whispered in the ear of the lonely. The wicked and the proud tremble at its warnings, but to the wounded and the penitent it has a mother's voice. The wilderness and the solitary place have been made glad by it, and the fire on the hearth has lit the reading of its wellworn page. It has woven itself into our dearest dreams; so that love, friendship, sympathy and devotion, memory and hope, put on the beautiful garments of its treasured speech, breathing of frankincense and myrrh. No man is poor or desolate who has this treasure for his own. When the landscape darkens and the trembling pilgrim comes to the Valley named of the Shadow, he is not afraid to enter; he takes the rod and staff of Scripture in his hand; he says to friend and comrade: "Good-bye, we shall meet again," and comforted by that support, he goes toward the lonely pass as one who walks through darkness into light.

Henry Van Dyke.

BIBLE STUDY COURSE

OLD TESTAMENT

INTRODUCTORY LESSON

"I attend church, and do what I can for the church, because I believe in it. I have found nothing in my religion that has interferred with my progress for a single moment. I have never been held back from a single opportunity. It has been my source of inspiration and strength, and comfort, and I should be an ingrate and a fool to desert it. Criticized and mocked, as it is at times, yet the church stands for all that is finest in our thoughts. It is still the mother of our greatest sons and daughters."—*Edgar Guest.*

TO THE STUDENT:

When you open the Bible for study, you finger the pages of one of the oldest complete documents known to the literary world. It is, in fact, a small library, a set of sixty-six books in one volume, written by at least thirty-six men over a period of 1,600 years. You should study this volume with eagerness, for it holds within its sacred covers the historical facts and the religious development of that race of people whom God chose to weave the pattern of life for the Christian world to follow throughout the ages.

It will be invaluable to you as a student if during the course you will picture these Hebrews of old as being real people. They knew their land just as you know yours. They were at home and at ease just as you are in your city and community. They dressed in the style of their day just as you observe the styles of today, and spoke their language just as you speak English. They loved and hated, married, had homes and families, lived in cities and on farms, worked and played, fought wars, and knew sorrow. They lived with all the emotion that we live with now. Realizing these truths, it will be easy for you to span the years between, and realize that they have given us through the Old Testament an infallible proof of a personal God and a living Christ.

While there are sixty-six books in this one volume, they are unified in the person of Christ whose coming was prophesied in the first book of the Old Testament. As you study the lives of these Hebrew people, you will be conscious of a feeling of expectancy which existed throughout the Old Testament period and which had its fulfillment in Jesus Christ. The Mosaic Law and the Gospel met in Him, for he said of himself, "Think not that I am come to destroy the law or the prophets: I am not come to destroy but to fulfill."

You should not be disturbed because there are no original manuscripts of this great book. The original manuscripts of many of our famous pieces of literature have disappeared. Even a first edition of *Alice in Wonderland* is not known to be in existence. John Bunyan destroyed the original of *Pilgrim's Progress,* and years later in remorse rewrote it. The Bible was copied and recopied by pen for centuries before printing was invented, and we accept these handmade copies or reprints just as we accept a publisher's edition today.

As you continue your study, you will find that there is no quarrel between the Bible and science. The Bible unequivocally makes the universe the work of a personal God. The greatest scientists, devout believers in God, make no valid objection to this claim, but add the support of their positive testimony. It is a striking fact, too, that the findings of modern science closely parallel the order of creation as stated in the first chapter of Genesis. Eminent geologists emphatically declare the scheme of creation is so perfect as to preclude any other conclusion.

The Introduction and the Appendix to this text will be helpful to you, in that they set up not only the standards and requirements of the course, but also give you little glimpses into the greatness of the Bible. From these materials and the quotations about the Bible, which are interspersed throughout the course, you will see how some of the world's greatest leaders have regarded the Book and how they have valued its influence in their lives. You will see, too, how it is related to geography and world history and what a place it holds in the field of literature. And most important of all, you will come to realize more and more that it has great cultural and personal value.

Questions

1. What impressions do you gain from this article as to the value of a knowledge of the Bible? Enumerate the main points in the article.

2. Discuss a few of the quotations contained in this book of what great men have said about the Bible. Which quotation do you like best?

3. Name several particulars in which the Bible differs from all other books. (See II Timothy 3:16-17, and II Peter 1:21.)

4. Give a few quotations from the Bible itself to show its importance to man. "Search the scriptures. . . . ." (See John 5:39.)

5. Can a person be really educated without a knowledge of the Bible?

6. What are some of the chief contributions of the church (or churches) to the community? Would you like to live in a community where there are no churches? Why? What do you think is the chief mission of the church?

7. What are your reasons for taking this course, and in what spirit are you undertaking it? Mention some of the cultural and spiritual values that should result from a study of the Bible. This course should give you not just factual information about the Bible but, more important, inspiration and spiritual growth.

8. Memorize II Tim. 2:15, 3:16 and II Peter 1:21.

Suggestions:

1. At the outset make sure that you understand the plan of the course and the requirements for credit— standards to be met, minimum requirements, memory passages, quotations, final examinations, etc. You should not overlook the special articles in the "Appendix," which are to be studied in connection with lessons on which these articles have a bearing.

2. As you proceed with the course, you should try to relate the lessons studied by making systematic reviews and summaries; and try to find the great spiritual teachings of the lessons. The course requires application and real study, but it should afford you genuine pleasure and profit.

3. You should own a personal copy of the Bible and not hesitate to mark in it passages which impress you as having great value. You should, also keep a good note-book.

I. Early Period

Introduction. The record of this period of "beginnings," which extends in time through the settlement of the Hebrews in Egypt, is contained in the book of Genesis. The term *genesis* means "beginning" and is applied to the first book of the Bible because this book contains an account of the beginnings of things. In it are found the earliest stories of Hebrew literature. Genesis has two main divisions—Chapters 1-11 and 12-50. The first division, extending in point of time from the beginning to the call of Abraham, gives the account of creation and tells "the beginnings of life" men saw in operation around them: the beginnings of the universe, plant, animal, and human life; agriculture, sheep, and cattle-raising; iron and metal work; musical instruments; family life and worship; sacrifice, sin, hatred, and murder; Divine judgment and Divine covenant with man. The second division, Chaps. 12-50, relates to the Patriachal Period, which follows in the next chapter. (See *Introduction* to this period, page 10.)

---

1. The Creation

1. Note carefully Genesis 1:1 and read in connection with it Psalm 19:1-5 and Psalm 104.

2. Make a list by days of things created as reported in Genesis 1.

3. Was God alone in the creation? Genesis 1:26; John 1:1-3; Hebrew 1:1-2.

4. What was God's first positive law to man? Genesis 2:16-17.

5. Man was to perform what double duty? Genesis 2:15.

6. Give an account of the creation of woman and the institution of marriage. Genesis 2:18-25.

7. What name did Adam give his wife and why? Genesis 3:20.

8. Quotations (to be written in pupil's notebook)[1]
   a. "Let there be light." Genesis 1:3.
   b. "And God saw everything that he had made, and, behold it was very good." Genesis 1:31.
   c. "I will make an helpmeet for him." Genesis 2:18.
9. Locate the Tigris and Euphrates Rivers.
10. Commit to memory Genesis 1:1 and the names of the books of law (Genesis, Exodus, Leviticus, Numbers, Deuteronomy).
11. Learn the meanings of *Bible, Pentateuch, Torah, Canon, Covenant, Testament, Exodus, Genesis, Leviticus, Numbers, Deuteronomy, Adam, Eve, firmament.* See GLOSSARY.

2. The Temptation

1. Give a brief account of the Temptation. Genesis 3:1-6.
2. Note the three human desires appealed to in Genesis 3:6 and compare with I John 2:16.
3. What human trait did Adam and Eve show in yielding to temptation?
4. How did they try to evade responsibility?
5. What is the first prophecy concerning the coming of the Christ? Genesis 3:15.
6. How was Adam punished for his sin? Genesis 3:17-19, 23-24.
7. What follows yielding to temptation? Genesis 3:17, 22-24; Romans 6:23; James 1:15.
8. How did Jesus overcome temptation? Matthew 4:4-10.

[1]The quotations given in connection with each lesson, together with others selected by the teacher or the pupil, are to be written in the pupil's notebook, with such explanation or comment as will make the setting and meaning clear. Usually the pupil should write the name of the speaker, the one spoken to and the purpose of the speaker or the condition under which the message was spoken. For example, Genesis 4:9: "Am I my brother's keeper?" This was spoken by Cain to the Lord in answer to the Lord's inquiry about Cain's brother Abel.

Note: Pupils should be able to complete a quotation when part of it is given or be able to fill in missing words.

9. Quotations:
   a. "The woman whom thou gavest to be with me, she gave me of the tree, and I did eat." Genesis 3:12.
   b. "In the sweat of thy face shalt thou eat bread." Genesis 3:19.
   c. "Dust thou art, and unto dust shalt thou return." Genesis 3:19.
   Commit to memory the above quotations.
10. Learn the meaning of *cherubim*. See GLOSSARY.

3. Cain, Abel, and Enoch

1. What were the occupations of Cain and Abel? Genesis 4:2.
2. Why was Abel's offering accepted and Cain's rejected? Genesis 4:3-7; Hebrews 11:4; Romans 10:17.
3. What resulted from Cain's jealousy? Genesis 4:8.
4. What was Cain's punishment for the murder of his brother? Genesis 4:9-15.
5. After Abel's death who became Adam's successor in the godly line? Genesis 4:25-26.
6. What is said about Enoch in Genesis 5:21-24; Hebrews 11:5; Jude 1:14-15?
7. Commit to memory:
   a. "Am I my brother's keeper?" Genesis 4:9.
   b. "The voice of thy brother's blood crieth unto me from the ground." Genesis 4:10.
8. Learn the meanings of the following terms: *altar, offering, oracle*.

4. The Flood

1. What reason is here given for the flood? Genesis 6:1-7, 11-13.
2. What were Noah's distinguishing traits? Genesis 6:8-9; 7:1; Hebrews 11:7; II Peter 2:5.
3. What did God tell Noah to do? Genesis 6:14-21.
4. Give the dimensions of the ark and other specifications concerning its structure. Genesis 6:15-16.

5. How long did it take Noah to build it? Genesis 5:32, 7:6.
6. Who were saved? What animals did God instruct Noah to take? Genesis 7:1-3, 13-14.
7. How long were Noah and his family in the ark? Genesis 7:11, 24, 8:13-16.
8. What was the extent of the destruction? Genesis 7:21-23.
9. What was the first duty Noah performed after leaving the ark? Genesis 8:20.
10. What is the significance of the rainbow? Genesis 9:12-17.
11. Quotations:
   a. "While the earth remaineth, seed time and harvest, and cold and heat, and summer and winter, and day and night shall not cease." Genesis 8:22.
   b. "I do set my bow in the cloud." Genesis 9:13.
   c. "My spirit shall not always strive with man." Genesis 6:3.
12. Locate *Mt. Ararat.*

---

5. The Origin of the Races, the Tower of Babel, and the Confusion of Tongues

Introduction. After the flood, the three sons of Noah and their families, according to God's plan, scattered to the known parts of the earth, giving origin to the various races. Japheth's descendants, occupying the Mediterranean coast lands, and Asia eastward to Media, became the Europeans (Genesis 10:1-5.) The descendants of Ham, taking possession of Abyssinia, northern Africa, and Babylon, gave origin to the colored races (Genesis 10:6-20.) The children of Shem, inhabiting the land of Arabia and southeastern Asia, became the Hebrews, Arabians, Assyrians, and Persians, all of whom speak the Semitic languages. (Genesis 10:21-32.)

1. What great hunter was the founder of the city of Babylon? Genesis 10:8-10.
2. Give an account of the building of the Tower of Babel, listing three purposes. Genesis 11:1-9.
3. What were two results? Genesis 11:1, 5-9.
4. Quotation:
   "So the Lord scattered them abroad from thence upon the face of all the earth." Genesis 11:8.
5. Locate: Babylon, Media, Arabia, Armenia, Assyria.
6. Explain the term, *Babel.* See GLOSSARY.

II. The Patriarchal Period.

Introduction. This period covers about 500 years, extending in point of time from the migration of Abraham to the birth of Moses. It is chiefly concerned with the history of the four patriarchs: Abraham, Isaac, Jacob, and Joseph. The narratives are found in the second division of Genesis, Chapters 12-50. Note the biographical nature of these narratives.

NOTE: See "Important Peoples of Bible Times," pages 63-64.

6. Abraham and Lot

1. Locate Abraham's early home. Genesis 11:31.
2. What did God command Abraham to do? Genesis 12:1.
3. Why did Abraham and Lot separate? Genesis 13:5-12.
4. What encouragement did God give him? Genesis 13:14-17.
5. In the following readings what incidents illustrate Abraham's unselfishness, benevolence, obedience, belief in prayer: Genesis 12:4, 13:9, 14:20, 18:23-33.
6. Quotations:
   a. "Get thee out of thy country, and from thy kindred." Genesis 12:1.
   b. "Shall not the judge of all the earth do right?" Genesis 18:25.
7. Locate on the map the following places: *Ur, Haran, Chaldea, Babylonia, Mesopotamia, Canaan, Shechem, Bethel, Hebron, Damascus.*
8. Draw a map showing Abraham's wanderings.
9. Explain the following terms and names: *Patriarch, monotheism, polytheism, Promised Land, Palestine, Abram, Abraham, Hebrew.*

7. Abraham and His Sons

1. Why and when was Abraham's name changed? Genesis 17:1-8.
2. What law did God give Abraham and his descendants? Genesis 17:10-13.
3. How did God show his sympathy when Hagar was cast out? Genesis 21:12-20.

4. What was God's promise concerning Ishmael? Genesis 16:12, 17:20.

5. What people today claim to be descendants of Ishmael? See GLOSSARY.

6. How was Abraham's faith tested? Genesis 18:10-15, 22:1-6.

7. Note the dialogue between Abraham and Isaac. Genesis 22:7-8. Copy this in your notebook.

8. How was Isaac's life spared? Genesis 22:9-13.

9. Write a synopsis of the romance of Isaac and Rebekah. Genesis 24.

10. What is significant about each of the following? *Machpelah* (Gen. 22:2, 23:19), *Mt. Moriah.*

8. Jacob and Esau

1. How did the brothers, Jacob and Esau, differ physically and temperamentally? Genesis 25:20-27.

2. How did Jacob take advantage of Esau's hunger? Genesis 25:29-34.

3. For what pittance did Esau sell his birthright? What modern applications might be made?

4. How and why did Rebekah and Jacob deceive Isaac? Genesis 27:1-33.

5. Why was Jacob compelled to flee? Genesis 27:41-45, 28:1-5.

6. Quotations:
   a. "Esau despised his birthright." Genesis 25:34.
   b. "The voice is Jacob's voice, but the hands are the hands of Esau." Genesis 27:22.

7. Explain the following: *Edom, Edomites.*

9. Jacob, Rachel, and Laban

1. Describe the place and nature of Jacob's dream. Genesis 28:10-19.

2. What vow did Jacob make? Genesis 28:20-22.

3. Under what conditions did Jacob meet Rachel? Genesis 29:1-12.

4. How did Laban deceive Jacob? Genesis 29:15-26.

5. How did Jacob trick Laban in retaliation?
   Genesis 30:25-43.
6. Jacob, alarmed at the approach of Esau, resorts to what
   measures? Genesis 32:9-12.
7. Why and when was Jacob's name changed to Israel?
   Genesis 32:24-28.
8. Give an account of his meeting with Esau.
   Genesis 33:1-16.
9. Compare the following promises: Genesis 28:14, 12:2-3,
   26:2-5. Copy these in your notebook.
10. Give the names of the twelve sons of Jacob. Genesis
    35:23-26. The names of these men are important,
    since they will become later the heads of the Twelve
    Tribes. See p. 75.
11. Quotations:
    a. "Surely the Lord is in this place; and I knew it not."
       Genesis 28:16.
    b. "They seemed unto him but a few days, for the love
       he had to her." Genesis 29:20.
    c. "The Lord watch between me and thee, when we are
       absent one from another." Genesis 31:49.
12. Explain the meaning of the following: *Bethel, Mizpah,
    Haran, Jacob, Israel, tithe.*

10. Joseph and His Troubles

Read Genesis 37 and 39; Psalm 105:17-22.
1. Why did Joseph's brothers hate him?
2. What were some results of this hatred?
3. What was the significance of Joseph's dreams?
   Genesis 37:5-11.
4. Why was Joseph cast into prison in Egypt?
5. Quotations:
   a. "Israel loved Joseph more than all his children."
      Genesis 37:3.
   b. "Behold this dreamer cometh." Genesis 37:19.
   c. "A coat of many colors." Genesis 37:3.

11. Joseph and His Success

Read Genesis 40-45.
1. Describe the dreams of the butler and the baker, and
   give Joseph's interpretations.

2. What was Joseph's interpretation of Pharaoh's dream?
3. What position did Joseph receive?
4. What events led to the settlement of Joseph's brethren and Jacob in Egypt?
5. How many years did Joseph spend in bondage? Genesis 37:2, 41:46.
6. The incidents related in the following references indicate that Joseph possessed what Christ-like qualities? Genesis 45:15, 46:29, 50:19-21.
7. Quotations:
   a. "Bring down my gray hairs with sorrow to the grave." Genesis 42:38.
   b. "God did send me before you to preserve life." Genesis 45:5.
8. Locate Goshen and the Nile River. See GLOSSARY.
9. Explain the meaning of *Pharaoh*.

---

12. The Book of Job

The Book of Job is generally considered one of the great literary masterpieces of the world. Tennyson pronounced it "the greatest poem whether of ancient or modern time." Carlyle said of it, "There is nothing written in the Bible or out of it of equal literary merit."

Job is studied in connection with the Patriarchal Period because the events of the book are thought to have occurred during the Patriarchal Period.

The theme of the Book of Job is the problem of human suffering or more specifically the reason why the righteous and innocent must suffer. No final solution is given this problem, but the book does show the spirit in which suffering and adversity should be met.

The book is artistically constructed and contains some of the deepest thought and sublimest poetry that has come down to us from ancient times. Scholars differ as to whether the Book of Job should be regarded as history or parable. The authorship of Job has been ascribed by different scholars to Job himself, Moses, Solomon, Isaiah, Hezekiah, Baruch; but the real author is unknown. The prologue and epilogue are in prose, and the rest of the book is in poetry. The entire book forms a sublime drama.

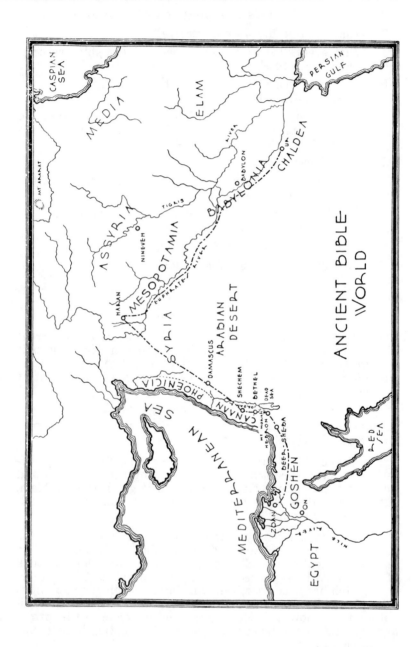

The outline of the Book of Job comprises four main divisions: (1) the prologue, (2) the arguments, (3) the conclusion, and (4) the epilogue.

1. The Prologue, 1, 2:1-10.
   a. Where did Job live? 1:1.
   b. What do we learn of Job's character from 1:1, 8?
   c. How many children did he have? 1:2.
   d. How prosperous and prominent was he? 1:3.
   e. Did Job believe in family religion? 1:4, 5.
   f. What disasters befell Job? 1:13-19.
   g. How did Job react under these disasters?   1:20-22, 2:3, 9, 10.

2. The Arguments, chs. 2:11-13; 32-37.
   a. What three friends came to comfort Job and mourn with him seven days and nights? 2:11-13.
   b. Who else joined in condemning Job? Chs. 32-37.

3. The Conclusion, chs. 38-41, 42:1-9.
   a. Who *finally* spoke and convinced Job of his inability to know the answer to his problems? Chs. 38-40.
   b. How did Job show his penitence? 42:1-9 (especially verse 6).

4. The Epilogue, 42:10-17.
   What was the final reward of Job's faithfulness? 42:10-17.

5. Quotations:
   a. "Satan came also among them." 1:6.
   b. "Canst thou by searching find out God?" 11:7.
   c. "Though He slay me, yet will I trust Him." 13:15.
   d. "If a man die, shall he live again?" 14:14.

6. Define the following terms: *prologue, epilogue.*

Read *Literary Types,* "Literary Characteristics of the Bible" by Dr. Umphrey Lee, page 67.

III. Early National Period.

Introduction. This period extends from the birth of Moses to the establishment of the monarchy under Saul, a span of about 500 years. Early in the period the Israelites were led out of Egypt under Moses, where they had remained for 430 years. Their numbers had increased from a few hundred at the time of Joseph to more than two million at the time of the exodus. Some authorities place the number as high as three million. For many generations the Hebrews were treated with great kindness by the Egyptians, but finally their prosperity and rapid increase in population aroused the fear of the Egyptian rulers who took away all their property and made slaves of them. Moses was called of God to deliver them from this great oppression. Under his leadership they left Egypt and started for Canaan, their long-sought "promised land." However, because of their military and spiritual unpreparedness, they were not permitted to go directly into Canaan by the shorter northern route; but were, after crossing the Red Sea, turned to the south into the desert areas of the great peninsula of Sinai and regions to the northwest where they spent forty years in wanderings. During their "sojourn and wanderings" all the older generation with the exception of Joshua and Caleb died. Under Joshua, Moses' able successor, the Israelites finally entered Canaan, their promised new home. But before they could really possess this new home they had to conquer the native inhabitants. Thus they "passed from an unorganized group of tribes to a settled nation and from a nomadic people to a race engaged in agricultural and urban pursuits."

---

13. Moses

Read Exodus 1, 2, 3, 4:1-20.

1. Why and how were the Hebrews persecuted?
2. What events were connected with Moses's early history?
3. What caused him to flee to Midian?
4. Tell the story of Moses's call and his excuses.

5. Moses' life is divided into three equal periods. What was the extent of each period and where was each spent?

6. Quotations:

   a. "There arose up a new king over Egypt which knew not Joseph." Ex. 1:8.

   b. "The place whereon thou standest is holy ground." Ex. 3:5.

   c. "A land flowing with milk and honey." Ex. 3:8.

7. Locate Rameses, Midian. See map, page 26, and GLOSSARY.

14. The Plagues

Read Exodus 5-12.

1. How did the Egyptians increase the oppression of the Hebrews?

2. Why did the Children of Israel at first refuse to hear Moses? See Ex. 4:31; 6:9.

3. How did Moses and Aaron seek to convince Pharaoh?

4. What was the convincing feature of the third plague?

5. Which of the ten plagues finally brought about the deliverance of the Hebrews? Exodus 12:13.

6. What important Jewish feast originated at this time? Exodus 12:13, 13:3-10.

7. Quotations:

   a. "This is the finger of God." Exodus 8:19.

   b. "Let my people go." Exodus 10:3.

8. Define *plague, miracle, Passover, Exodus.*

15. The Exodus

1. Why would it have been unwise for the Hebrews to march through the land of the Philistines? Exodus 13:17.

2. How were the people assured of Divine presence? Exodus 13:21-22.

3. Describe the Egyptian pursuit and the escape of the Hebrews at the Red Sea. Exodus 14:5-31.

4. Quotations:

   a. "He took not away the pillar of cloud by day, nor the pillar of fire by night." Exodus 13:22.

   b. "The Lord shall fight for you, and ye shall hold your peace." Exodus 14:14.

5. Commit to memory the names of the books of history (Joshua, Judges, Ruth, I Samuel, II Samuel, I Kings, II Kings, I Chronicles, II Chronicles, Ezra, Nehemiah, and Esther).

6. Trace the journey of the Hebrews from the Red Sea to the Jordan, locating all important places shown on the map, page 26.

16. Wilderness Experiences

1. How were food and water provided for the Hebrews? Give specific instances. Exodus 15:23-25, 16:4-5.

2. What enemy attacked the Hebrews in the wilderness, and how were they defeated? Exodus 17:8-13.

3. What advice did Jethro give to Moses? Exodus 18:13-26.

4. Describe the sending of the spies, and tell what they reported. Numbers 13:17-33.

5. Tell the story of Balaam and Balak. Numbers 22, 23, 24, and 31.

6. Give an account of the death and burial of Moses. Deuteronomy 32:48-52; 34:5-7.

7. Why was Moses called the great emancipator and the great law-giver?

8. Who succeeded Moses as leader of the Israelites? Deuteronomy 34:8-9; Numbers 27:18-23.

9. Where and how were the ten commandments given? Exodus 19-20; 31:18; 32:15-19.; 34:1, 4, 27, 28.

10. Commit to memory the Ten Commandments. Exodus 20:1-17.

    a. Thou shalt have no other gods before Me.

    b. Thou shalt not make unto thee any graven image, or any likeness of any thing . . . Thou shalt not bow down thyself to them, nor serve them . . .

c. Thou shalt not take the name of the Lord thy God in vain: for the Lord will not hold him guiltless that taketh his name in vain.

d. Remember the Sabbath day to keep it holy. Six days shalt thou labor and do all thy work. But the seventh day is the sabbath of the Lord thy God: in it thou shalt not do any work. . . .

e. Honor thy father and thy mother: that thy days may be long upon the land which the Lord thy God giveth thee.

f. Thou shalt not kill.

g. Thou shalt not commit adultery.

h. Thou shalt not steal.

i. Thou shalt not bear false witness against thy neighbor.

j. Thou shalt not covet . . . any thing that is thy neighbor's.

11. Are the Commandments still binding on Christians? How did Jesus summarize these Commandments? Matt. 22:37-40. Commit to memory.

12. Quotations:

a. "Let us go up at once, and possess it; for we are well able to overcome it." Numbers 13:30.

b. "We were in our own sight as grasshoppers." Numbers 13:33.

c. "What hath God wrought!" Numbers 23:23.
   NOTE: This was the first message flashed over the telegraph wire by Samuel F. B. Morse in May, 1844.

d. "The Lord bless thee and keep thee:

   The Lord make his face shine upon thee, and be gracious unto thee:

   The Lord lift up his countenance upon thee, and give thee peace." Numbers 6:24-26. *Note:* This is a required memory passage.

13. Define *decalogue, manna, Sabbath.*

14. Locate on the map Sinai and Kadesh-barnea. Why is each important in the wilderness experiences? See GLOSSARY.

17. The Tabernacle

Read Exodus 25-30.

1. What was the Tabernacle? (Exodus 25:8.) Why was it erected? See "Development of Places of Worship," a note following Lesson 25, page 33.

2. Where and how did Moses receive the plans and specifications for the Tabernacle? Exodus 24:15-16.

3. How were the materials obtained for its building? Exodus 25:1-7.

4. Describe the apartments of the Tabernacle: the Court, the Holy Place, and the Holy of Holies.

5. Name and give the use of the articles of furniture found in each apartment.

6. Describe the Ark of the Covenant and tell what treasures it contained.

7. Who were chosen to be the priests, and how were they selected? Exodus 28:1, 40:15; Numbers 17:1-10.

8. The *sacrifice,* a vitally important part of Jewish worship, was an offering presented to God on His sacred altar by one invested with priestly power.[1]

   a. The burnt offering. Leviticus 1:2-9, 6:8-13.

   b. The meal offering. Leviticus 2:1-16, 6:14-23.

   c. The peace offering. Leviticus 3:1-17.

   d. The sin offering. Leviticus 4:1-35, 5:1-13, 6:24-30.

   e. The trespass offering. Leviticus 5:1-19, 6:2-7.

9. The feasts, observed annually, celebrated some great event or blessing.

   a. *The Feast of the Passover,* the first of the three great annual feasts, was observed in March or April, commemorating the Exodus which meant to the Hebrews freedom from bondage and the birth of

---

[1]After 70 A.D. when Titus destroyed the Temple, animal sacrifice ceased, leaving prayer as the one means of communication with God.

their nation. The Passover was to them what Independence Day is to the Americans. In a stricter sense, it commemorates the sparing of the Hebrews when the death angel passed over the land of bondage, smiting all the Egyptian first-born. Exodus 12:1-51; Leviticus 23:5; Deuteronomy 16:1-6.

b. *The Feast of the Pentecost*, the second of the annual feasts, was observed in June, commemorating the giving of the law on Mt. Sinai. It was called the "feast of weeks" because it was celebrated seven complete weeks after the Passover. A prominent feature of this one-day festival was the offering of two loaves of bread made from the first fruit of the wheat harvest. Leviticus 23:15-22.

c. *The Feast of Tabernacles*, the third of the annual feasts, was a thanksgiving for the autumn harvest of produce and fruits and a commemoration of God's watchful care during the wilderness experiences when they lived in fragile tents. It was observed in October and was somewhat like the American Thanksgiving season. Leviticus 23:39-43.

10. The *fast* was frequently practiced by the Jews as a religious duty in times of distress and humiliation. Through total abstinence from food and other indulgences they hoped to secure a more perfect spiritual communion with God. Usually the one who fasted rent or tore his garments and dressed in sackcloth and covered his head with ashes. It lasted from "even to even." The only national fast commanded in the Mosaic Law was the Day of Atonement.

The Day of Atonement, observed October 10, was the holiest day of the Jewish calendar. It was commanded to be not only a day of fasting but also a day of "Sabbath rest." It was the one day of the year when the High Priest was permitted to enter the Holy of Holies, where he performed certain sacred rites for the atonement of the sins of Israel. Leviticus 16, 23:27-32.

THE PLAN OF THE TABERNACLE

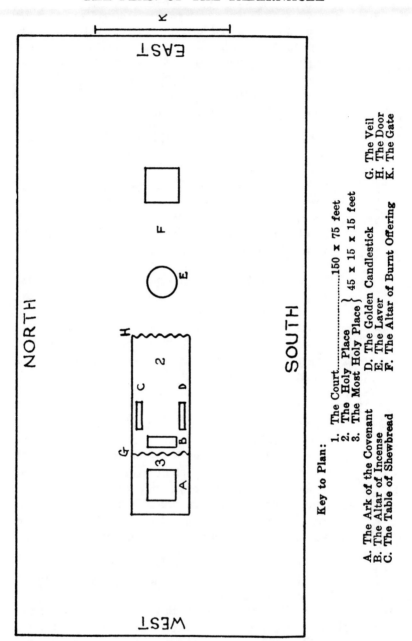

Key to Plan:

1. The Court .... 150 x 75 feet
2. The Holy Place ⎫ 45 x 15 x 15 feet
3. The Most Holy Place ⎭

A. The Ark of the Covenant   D. The Golden Candlestick   G. The Veil
B. The Altar of Incense   E. The Laver   H. The Door
C. The Table of Shewbread   F. The Altar of Burnt Offering   K. The Gate

THE CAMP OF ISRAEL

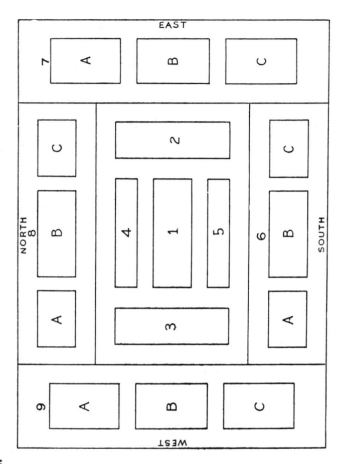

Key:

1. Tabernacle
2. Moses, Aaron, Priests
3. Gershon   (2,630) ⎫
4. Merari   (3,200) ⎬ Sons of Levi
5. Kohath   (2,720) ⎭
6. Camp Reuben
    A. Gad   (45,650)
    B. Reuben   (46,500)
    C. Simeon   (59,300)

7. Camp of Judah
    A. Issachar   (54,400)
    B. Judah   (74,600)
    C. Zebulon   (57,400)
8. Camp of Dan
    A. Asher   (41,500)
    B. Dan   (62,700)
    C. Naphtali   (53,400)
9. Camp of Ephraim
    A. Benjamin   (35,400)
    B. Ephraim   (40,500)
    C. Manasseh   (32,200)

NOTE: The number of fighting men totaled 603,550 at this time.

[23]

18. Conquest and Settlement of Canaan

1. What former incidents revealed the character of Joshua and Caleb? Exodus 17:9-14; Numbers 14:6-9, 20, 30, 38.

2. Tell the story of Rahab and the spies. Joshua 2.

3. Describe the crossing of the Jordan. Joshua 3:14-17.

4. Why and when did the manna cease? Exodus 16:35; Joshua 5:11-12.

5. Describe the capture of Jericho. Joshua 6:1-25.

6. Caleb showed his vigor and faithfulness in old age by asking for what inheritance? Joshua 14:10-14, 15:14.

7. Why did the Hebrews lose the first battle of Ai? Joshua 7.

8. Give an account of the capture of Ai. Joshua 8.

9 Name the cities of refuge and give their purpose. Deuteronomy 19:1-13; Joshua 20:7-9.

10. Quotations:
    a. "Be strong and of good courage." Joshua 1:6.
    b. "Hewers of wood and drawers of water." Joshua 9:23.
    c. "Choose you this day whom ye will serve . . . but as for me and my house, we will serve the Lord." Joshua 24:15.

11. Show on the map the division of Canaan among the tribes.

12. Locate Gilgal, Mt. Ebal, Mt. Nebo, Jericho, Hebron, Shechem. See map, page 28 and GLOSSARY.

---

19. The Time of the Judges

Introduction. The period of the judges covers about 450 years (Acts 13:20), extending from the death of Joshua to the accession of Saul, the first king. It is generally believed that Samuel wrote the book of Judges to demonstrate the hopeless state of a nation that tries to get along without God.

It is not at all strange that the Hebrews, who were completely surrounded by idolatrous people, began to engage in the worship of idols. For their heathen practices God permitted Israel to become the prey of the invading hordes. However, when life became unbearable, "they cried unto the Lord," remembering what he had done for them in times past.

The narrative then centers about the lives of the judges whom God raised up at successive intervals of oppression to lead the Israelites to freedom.

1. Summarize the events immediately following the death of Joshua. Judges 1:1-2, 10.

2. Who was Othniel and from what people did he deliver the Israelites? Judges 1:13, 3:7-11.

3. Write a brief account of Ehud's delivery of Israel from the oppression of the Moabites. Judges 3:12-30.

4. What great woman was enabled by divine guidance to defeat Jabin, the Canaanitish king? Relate the circumstances of this victory. Judges 4.

5. How did the Midianites oppress the Hebrews? How was Gideon called to deliver his people? Judges 6.

6. Why did God tell Gideon to reduce his army? How was he to select the best soldiers? What strategy did he use in his attack? What was the outcome? Judges 7:1-22.

7. Who delivered Israel from the Ammonites? What was his rash vow and how was it fulfilled? Judges 11.

8. List at least six tasks which Samson's herculean strength enabled him to perform? Judges 13, 14, 15, 16.

9. Quotations:

   a. "The stars in their courses fought against Sisera." Judges 5:20.

   b. "He wist not that the Lord was departed from him." Judges 16:20.

   c. "The sword of the Lord, and of Gideon." Judges 7:18.

10. Explain the terms *Nazarite, vow, judges.*

20. Samuel, the Last of the Judges

Introduction. Samuel, one of the most powerful figures in Hebrew history, was God's spokesman during that transitional period when the form of government was changing from a theocracy to a monarchy. He was the last and the greatest of all the judges, the first in the line of prophets, and the founder of the first school of prophets.

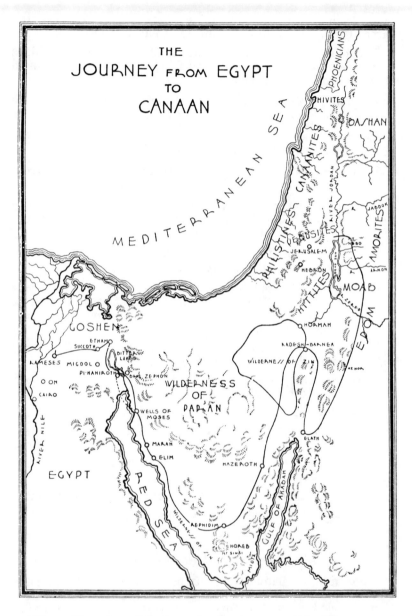

NOTE: There is a slight error in the above map. The line representing the probable route of wanderings should have been extended farther to the south to include Mt. Horeb. (Exodus 17:6; Deut. 5:2.)

1. Give a detailed account of the incidents in the early childhood of Samuel. I Samuel 1, 2.

2. How does it parallel the childhood of Jesus? I Samuel 2:26.

3. How was Samuel called to religious service? I Samuel 3:1-10.

4. What did God reveal to Samuel concerning the house of Eli? I Samuel 3:11-18.

5. List the tragedies which happened in connection with the Ark. Where was it finally placed and under whose care? I Samuel 4, 5, 6, 7:1-2; I Chronicles 15:28-29.

6. Samuel set up the stone, Ebenezer, as a memorial of God's help on what occasion? I Samuel 7:3-12.

7. What is said about Samuel as a prophet and as a circuit judge? I Samuel 3:19-21, 7:15-17.

8. Quotations:

   a. "Every man did that which was right in his own eyes." Judges 17:6.

   b. "Speak, for thy servant heareth." I Samuel 3:10. (Commit to memory.)

   c. "Be strong, and quit yourselves like men." I Samuel 4:9.

   d. "Hitherto hath the Lord helped us." I Samuel 7:12.

FIFTEEN JUDGES OF ISRAEL
(This material is for reference only)

Judges	People Against Whom Wars Were Waged	Biblical References
1. Othniel	Mesopotamians	Judges 3:7-10
(A nephew of Caleb)		
2. Ehud	Moabites	Judges 3:12-30
3. Shamgar	Philistines	Judges 3:31, 5:6
4. Deborah and Barak	Canaanites	Judges 4
5. Gideon	Midianites	Judges 6:1-8:32
(Zerubbabel)		
6. Abimelech	Civil War	Judges 9:22
(A son of Gideon)		
7. Tola	Civil War	Judges 10:1
8. Jair	Civil War	Judges 10:3-5
9. Jephthah	Ammonites	Judges 10:6-12:7
10. Ibzan	No peoples named	Judges 12:8-10
11. Elon	No peoples named	Judges 12:11-12
12. Abdon	No peoples named	Judges 12:13-14
13. Samson	Philistines	Judges 13-16
14. Eli	Philistines	I Samuel 1:1-4:18
(Judge and High Priest)		
15. Samuel	Philistines	I Samuel 7:3-12:25
(Judge and Prophet)		

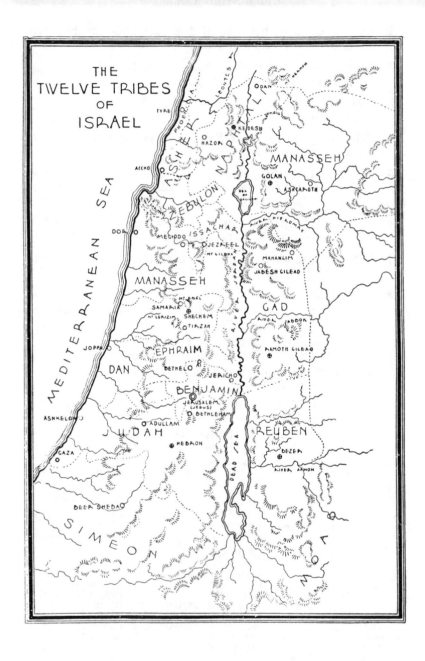

21. Ruth

Following the book of Judges comes the beautiful pastoral story of Ruth, a gentile woman who became one of the ancestors of Christ.

Read the entire book (four chapters).

1. Outline of the story:
   a. Elimelech's family goes to Moab. Ruth 1:1-5.
   b. The bereaved Naomi returns to Bethlehem accompanied by Ruth. Ruth 1:6-22.
   c. Ruth gleans in the fields of Boaz, a near kinsman of Elimelech. Ruth 2.
   d. Ruth becomes the wife of Boaz. Ruth 4:13.
   e. A son, Obed, is born. Ruth 4:13-16.
   f. Genealogy of David. Ruth 4:18-22.

2. Locate Moab and Bethlehem. See map, page 28 and GLOSSARY.

3. Quotations:
   a. "Whither thou goest, I will go; and where thou lodgest I will lodge; thy people shall be my people, and thy God my God." Ruth 1:16.
   b. "If aught but death part thee and me." Ruth 1:17.

4. Explain the terms *gentile, genealogy*.

IV. Monarchic Period.

Introduction. Israel desired a king who would be a military leader against the increasing pressure of external enemies, and who would also further the movement for unity among the tribes. At first Samuel took this as a personal affront against him as a judge, and also a sin against God, who was their King. Later he acceded to their wishes, apparently with the divine approval, and anointed Saul, the son of Kish, as king. This period covers about 500 years, extending from the anointing of Saul to the capture of Jerusalem by the Babylonians in 586 B.C. During the reign of Saul, David, and Solomon, the kingdom was a unity. After Solomon's reign it became two kingdoms, Judah (two tribes to the South) and Israel (ten tribes of the North).

During this period, and partly in the next, the prophets[1] played a conspicuous part in the life of the Hebrew people. The priest and the prophets differed considerably. The priest represented man to God in acts of penitence, sacrifice, and worship. The prophet represented God to man. The prophet was one who "spoke for God." As God's spokesman he might interpret the past, describe the present, and prophesy the future. The prophets of the Old Testament may be classified as follows: as regards *material,* major and minor; as regards *record,* written and oral; as regards *time,* pre-exilic (before the exile of Judah), exilic (during the exile), and post-exilic (after the exile). See the "Chart of Most Prominent Old Testament Prophets," page 49.

Notice the political and commercial position of Palestine. It was situated between the great nations of the ancient world and thus became the frequent battleground of contesting powers. It was on the main caravan routes between East and West, North and South, and thus prospered through trade.

22. The United Kingdom—Saul

1. For what *three* purposes did Israel desire a king? I Sam. 8:20.
2. Briefly describe the circumstances surrounding the anointing of Saul to be king over Israel. I Sam. 9, 10:1.
3. Describe Saul's physical appearance and character. I Sam. 9:2.
4. What was Saul's great sin? I Sam. 15:1-21.
5. What was the meaning of Samuel's rebuke to Saul in I Sam. 15:22-28?
6. Describe the moral degradation of Saul as shown in I Sam: 16:14-15.
7. Why did Saul so bitterly hate David? I Sam. 18:5-15, 28-29, 19:1, 9-11.
8. Who was Saul's distinguished son? I Sam. 14:1.

[1]Prophets are not peculiar to this period. In addition to the Major and Minor Prophets, many other Bible characters were endowed with the power of prophesying. Abraham was the first to be called a prophet (Gen. 20:7), although Enoch and Noah are represented in the New Testament as prophets (Jude 1:14, II Peter 2:25). Moses was a great prophet (Deut. 34:10). From the time of Samuel to the exile there were "schools of prophets" and a succession of prophets. Malachi was the last of the Old Testament prophets. After him no prophetic voice was heard until the appearance of John the Baptist, the forerunner of Christ. The New Testament gives numerous instances of the exercise of the gift of prophecy.

9. Tell briefly of the tragic deaths of Saul and Jonathan. I Sam. 31 and I Chron. 10:1-14.
10. Quotations:
    a. "Is Saul also among the prophets?" I Sam. 10:11.
    b. "God save the king." I Sam. 10:24.
    c. "To obey is better than sacrifice." I Sam. 15:22.

23. The United Kingdom—David

1. Tell of David's anointing by Samuel. I Sam. 16:6-13.
2. What is the difference between God's and man's judgment of persons? I Sam. 16:7.
3. Briefly outline David's combat with Goliath of Gath. I Sam. 17.
4. With whom did David form a great friendship, which has since become proverbial? I Sam. 18:1-4, 20:11-17.
5. How was David made King over all Israel, and what city did he capture and make the seat of his kingdom? II Sam. 5:1-5, 5:6-10.
6. How extensive was David's kingdom? II Sam. 8:1-18.
7. Why was David forbidden to build the Temple? II Sam. 7:1-11; I Chron. 17:1-15, 22:5-10, 28:2-3.
8. What great promises did God make to David? II Sam. 7:12-17; Isaiah 9:6-7; Luke 1:30-33; Acts 2:29-36.
9. Which three of the "Ten Commandments" did David break in II Sam. 11? See Ex. 20:1-17.
10. In what striking way did Nathan reveal the awfulness of David's sin to him? II Sam. 12:1-9.
11. Did God forgive David's sin? II Sam. 12:13; Psalm 32:1-2.
12. Which son of David rebelled against him and was killed? II Sam. 15:1-18, 18:9-17.
13. Quotations:
    a. "How are the mighty fallen!" II Sam. 1:19.
    b. "From Dan even to Beersheba." II Sam. 3:10.
    c. "Thou art the man." II Sam. 12:7.
14. Locate Adullum, Mt. Gilboa, and Philistia. See maps, pages 26 and 28, and Glossary.

24. The United Kingdom—Solomon

1. Why did Solomon choose wisdom? I Kings 3:5-9; II Chron. 1:7-10.
2. Pleased at Solomon's choice, what did God promise him and on what condition? I Kings 3:10-14.

3. What was Solomon's first demonstration of his great wisdom? I Kings 3:16-28.
4. What were some of the resources of Solomon? I Kings 10:14-15, 22.
5. Describe the palace of Solomon. I Kings 10:18-21.
6. How was Solomon regarded in the estimation of all people? Why? I Kings 10:24.
7. What famous queen visited Solomon, and what was her verdict? What gifts did she make him? I Kings 10:1-10.
8. What was the three-fold sin of Solomon? I Kings 11:1-3, 4-6, 7-8.
9. What was his consequent punishment for these sins? I Kings 11:11-13.
10. Quotations:
    a. "I am but a little child." I Kings 3:7.
    b. "The half was not told me." I Kings 10:7.

25. The Temple

Study I Kings 5, 6, 7, 8, 9. It is suggested that the student read all of the above chapters very carefully before attempting to answer the questions.

1. What charge did David give Solomon concerning the building of the Temple? I Chronicles 22, 6-11, 28:9-10, 20.
2. Where was the Temple located? Why? I Cronicles 21:8-27, and II Chronicles 3:1
3. What royal friend of David assisted Solomon in the building of the Temple, and in what way? I Kings 5:1-15.
4. What is said about the noise of the workmen during the building of the Temple? I Kings 6:7. What lesson may Christians learn from this in their work in the church today? I Thessalonians 4:11.
5. What is said about the construction of the Temple in I Kings 5:13-16, and I Chronicles 22:14.
6. What were the dimensions of the Temple proper? I Kings 6:2. How did this compare with the Tabernacle?
7. What was God's first promise to Solomon concerning the Temple? I Kings 6:12-13.
8. Describe the decorations on the inside walls of the Temple. I Kings 6:29.

9. What was the last thing that happened to the Tabernacle and its furniture? I Kings 8:1-9.
10. How did God show his approval of the Temple when the work was finished? I Kings 8:10-11.
11. Give a few extracts from Solomon's prayer of dedication. I Kings 8:12-66.
12. What was God's second promise to Solomon concerning the Temple? I Kings 9:1-9.
13. Quotation:
"I have built a house for the name of the Lord."
I Kings 8:20.
See the diagram of the ground plan of the Temple, on the following page.

Note: The following steps illustrate man's progressive development in the places of worship:

1. The altar
   a. This was the first and simplest place of worship. It was originally made of earth and unhewn stone, erected on sacred spots, especially high places.
   b. Noah built an altar when he left the Ark.
   c. Abraham and Jacob were great altar builders.

2. The Tabernacle
   This was a movable structure erected by the Hebrews while in the wilderness. The idea and the plans for its construction were given to Moses by Jehovah.

3. The Temple
   a. The idea of building the Temple originated with David.
   b. The first one was built in Jerusalem by Solomon, David's son.
   c. It was built after the pattern of the tabernacle, but twice the size, with more courts.
   d. Solomon's Temple was destroyed by Nebuchadnezzar and rebuilt by Zerubbabel. A third temple was built by Herod the Great. This temple was destroyed by Titus A.D. 70.

4. The Synagogue
   a. The synagogue probably originated during the Babylonian exile when the Jews had no place of worship.
   b. It was a place for instruction.
   c. It had no altar for sacrifice and the furnishings were simple.

5. The Church
   The church is the highest step upward in man's desire to worship.

GROUND PLAN OF THE TEMPLE

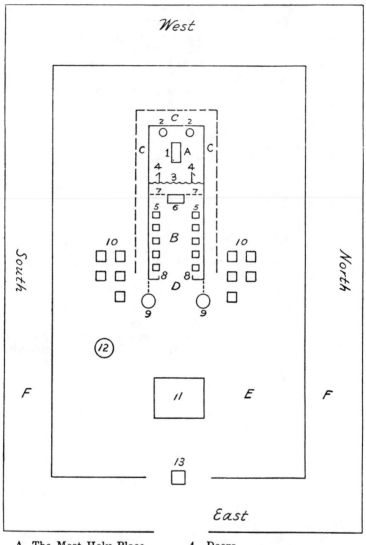

A. The Most Holy Place
B. The Holy Place
C. Space divided into rooms
D. The Porch
E. The Court of the Priests
F. The Court of the People
1. The Ark of the Covenant
2. The Cherubim
3. The Veil

4. Doors
5. Ten Tables of Shewbread
6. The Altar of Incense
7. The Golden Candlesticks
   (Five on each side)
8. Doors
9. Pillars, Jachin and Boaz
10. Lavers (five on each side)
11. Altar of Burnt Offering
12. The Molten Sea
13. The Pulpit

26. The Psalms

"The Psalms express the religious life of the Hebrew people and constitute the most wonderful collection of religious lyrics we possess." Luther called the Psalms "a Bible in miniature." The title, Psalms, is a Greek translation of a Hebrew word meaning *praises*. The term "Psalter," from the Greek word meaning *harp*, is another common name applied to the Psalms.

The editors of our Psalms, taking the principal collections as a basis and adding to them such other passages as were suitable for the Temple service of praise, formed them into a complete "Book of Praise" probably in the Maccabean Age— 2nd century B.C. This collection, called the Psalter, was used by the Jews as we use the modern hymn book today. The songs were sung to the music of the psaltery, an instrument of twelve strings, played upon by the fingers.

The Psalter was divided into five books, each closing with a doxology or *amen:*

I.	Psalms 1-41	IV.	Psalms 90-106
II.	Psalms 42-72	V.	Psalms 107-150
III.	Psalms 73-89		

Of all the books of the Old Testament the Psalter is most frequently quoted in the New Testament. Christians in all ages have made large use of the Psalms in public worship and in private devotion. "Preeminent among the books of the Old Testament, they are intended not for one age but for all time, and should be studied in the light of eternal truth, and local significance should be lost in the universal." The leading topic is *trouble* and *its relief.* As to sentiment, the classes are many and varied.

Hebrew poetry[1] has neither rhyme nor meter as is found in English poetry, but it does abound in rhythm,—rhythm in structure and rhythm in thought. Parallelism is its chief characteristic.[2]

The Psalms are predominantly lyric; however, a few may be classified as didactic.

1. Read the following Psalms for a study of parallelism: 19:7-10, 24, 115, and 30:5.

2. For what special purpose did David use Psalm 24?

---

[1] For a fuller discussion of Hebrew poetry, see Dr. Lee's article, "Literary Characteristics of the Bible," pages 67-70.

[2] Parallelism may be "synonymous," in which two successive lines deal with the same thought; "antithetic," in which the two lines contrast; "synthetic," in which the second line completes the thought of the first by an ascending rhythm; "constructive," in which the second line completes the first by means of some change of expression.

3. Each Psalm may be given a subject, such as "God's glory revealed in nature," "Trust," "Praise," "God's Word" (the Law), "Messianic," "Pardon," "Unity," and "Penitence." Read the following Psalms and write in your notebook after each Psalm one of the above subjects:

a. Psalm 119   e. Psalm 150   h. Psalm 51
b. Psalm 91   f. Psalm 100   i. Psalm 133
c. Psalm 19   g. Psalm 23   j. Psalm 32
d. Psalm 22

4. Quotations:
   a. "The Heavens declare the glory of God, and the firmament showeth his handiwork." Psalm 19:1.
   b. "The fear of the Lord is the beginning of wisdom." Psalm 111:10. See also Proverbs 9:10.
   c. "Thy word is a lamp unto my feet, and a light unto my path." Psalm 119:105.
   d. "Commit thy way unto the Lord; trust also in him; and he shall bring it to pass." Psalm 37:5.
   e. "Create in me a clean heart, O God; and renew a right spirit within me." Psalm 51:10.
   f. "Let the words of my mouth, and the meditation of my heart, be acceptable in thy sight, O Lord, my strength, and my redeemer." Psalm 19:14.
   g. "Be still, and know that I am God." Psalm 46:10.
   h. "Thy word have I hid in mine heart, that I might not sin against thee." Psalm 119:11.
   i. "Behold, how good and how pleasant it is for brethren to dwell together in unity!" Psalm 133:1.

5. Commit to memory Psalms 1, 19:14, 23, 91:1-2, and 100.

6. Commit to memory the names of the "Poetical Books" (Job, Psalms, Proverbs, Ecclesiastes, Song of Solomon).

7. Define *Psalter.*

---

27. *Proverbs, Ecclesiastes, and Song of Solomon*

Introductory Statement. Solomon was evidently the author of Ecclesiastes and the Song of Solomon and most of Proverbs. See Eccles. 1:1-12; Song of Sol. 1:1; Prov. 1:1, 30:1, 31:1.

1. *Proverbs.* The Book of Proverbs is a collection of wise sayings or maxims. A *proverb* is a brief expression of some practical wisdom.

    a. From what insect can we learn industry and thrift?
6:6-11, 30:25.

    b. According to 20:1, 23:20-21, 29-35, and 31:4-7, why is
it unwise to drink intoxicating liquors?

    c. What is so fittingly described in 31:10-31?

    d. Define *proverb*.

2. *Ecclesiastes.* "The burden of Ecclesiastes is the vanity of
life." The word *Ecclesiastes* means "the Preacher."

    a. According to Ecc. 1:2-3, what is the problem of Ecclesiastes?

    b. What is the message of 11:7-10 and 12:1 for youth?

    c. What did Solomon conclude "is the whole duty of
man"? 12:13-14.

3. *Song of Solomon.* This book "is a beautiful poem of loyalty and faithfulness." There are three leading interpretations of the book:

    a. Jewish—It teaches Jehovah's love for Israel.

    b. Christian—It portrays the mutual love between Christ
and His Church.

    c. It is a true story of Solomon's love for the Shulamite
maiden.

4. Quotations:

    a. "Cast thy bread upon the water: for thou shalt find it
after many days." Eccles. 11:1.

    b. "Righteousness exalteth a nation: but sin is a reproach
to any people." Prov. 14:34.

    c. "Train up a child in the way he should go: and when he
is old, he will not depart from it." Prov. 22:6.

    d. "A soft answer turneth away wrath." Prov. 15:1.

    e. "A wise son maketh a glad father." Prov. 10:1.

    f. "A good name is rather to be chosen than great riches."
Prov. 22:1.

    g. "Whatsoever thy hand findeth to do, do it with thy
might." Eccles. 9:10.

    h. "Keep thy heart with all diligence; for out of it are the
issues of life." Prov. 4:23.

    i. "Trust in the Lord with all thine heart; and lean not
unto thine own understanding. In all thy ways
acknowledge him, and he shall direct thy paths."
Proverbs 3:5-6.

5. Commit to memory Ecclesiastes 12:1, 12:13, and Prov.
3:5-6.

28. *The Divided Kingdom—Israel*

The Northern Kingdom

1. Why did Israel secede from the kingdom? I Kings 12:1-16: II Chron. 9:31, 10:1-15.
2. Whom did Israel make their king? I Kings 12:16-21.
3. Name four cities which were capitals of the Northern Kingdom at one time or another. I Kings 12:25; I Kings 16:23-24, 18:45, 21:1; II Kings 8:29.
4. In consequence of Ahab's sins, what dire prediction did Elijah make? I Kings 17:1.
5. What was Elijah's courageous reply to Ahab's false accusation? I Kings 18:1-2; 17-18.
6. What did Elijah propose to decide who is the true God? I Kings 18:19-25.
7. After Elijah's triumph, what was the verdict of the people? I Kings 18:26-40.
8. What was Ahab's sin against Naboth? How was it to be punished? I Kings 21:1-16, 21:17, 24, 22:29-38; II Kings 9:1-3, 11-37.
9. In what spectacular manner did Elisha succeed Elijah? II Kings 2:1-14.
10. What were the striking resemblances and differences between these two prophets? II Kings 1:8.
11. Give a detailed account of the healing of Naaman. II Kings 5.
12. Elisha is given credit for performing more miracles than any other prophet except Moses. List at least ten of these found in II Kings 2, 3, 4, 6, and 13.
13. Quotations:
    a. "My father also chastised you with whips, but I will chastise you with scorpions." I Kings 12:14.
    b. "A still small voice." I Kings 19:12.
    c. "A little cloud out of the sea, like a man's hand." I Kings 18:44.
    d. "As sheep that have not a shepherd." I Kings 22:17.
14. Define the terms: *Prophet, prophecy, prophesy, scorpions.*
15. Locate the following places: Mt. Carmel, Jezreel, Shechem, Samaria, Tirzah, and Damascus.

Statement. The Northern Kingdom, Israel, lasted 215 years, from 937 B.C. to 722 B.C., when it was overrun by Assyria and most of the Israelites taken away captives (Hurlbut). These ten tribes were never again restored to their land, and hence are called "the lost tribes."

29. *The Divided Kingdom—Israel (Concluded)*

1. What is the substance of Hosea's message?
   Hosea 4:1-2, 15-19.
2. Whom did God send from Judah to prophesy in Israel?
   Amos 1:1, 7:14-15.
3. To whom was Jonah sent and why was he displeased?
   Jonah 4:1-3.
4. What leads one to believe that Micah may have prophesied
   to both Judah and Israel? Micah 1:1.
5. Who carried Israel into captivity and where?
   II Kings 17:3-6.
6. Why did God permit the captivity of Israel?
   II Kings 17:7-17.
7. Upon what great city did Nahum pronounce doom?
   Nahum 1:1, 3:1, 5-7, 19.
8. Quotations:
   a. "Ephraim is joined to idols: let him alone."
      Hosea 4:17.
   b. "For I desired mercy, and not sacrifice; and the knowl-
      edge of God more than burnt offerings." Hosea 6:6.
   c. "For they have sown the wind, and they shall reap
      the whirlwind." Hosea 8:7.
   d. "Can two walk together, except they be agreed?"
      Amos 3:3.
9. Locate Assyria and the cities of Samaria, Shechem, Dan,
   and Bethel.
10. Memorize Micah 6:8 and the names of the books of the
    Major Prophets and Minor Prophets.
11. Explain the expression, *Lost Tribes.*

---

30. *The Divided Kingdom—Judah*

1. Did the people of Judah remain true to Jehovah during
   the reign of Rehoboam? I Kings 14:21-31.
2. According to I Kings 22:43-44, 46, what three good things
   characterize the reign of Jehosaphat and what one bad
   thing?
3. What three kings repaired the Temple in Jerusalem?
   II Chronicles 24:4-15, 29:1-12, 34:1-8.
4. What are the warnings and appeals Isaiah makes to Judah
   because of her sins? Isaiah 1:11-20, 2-11, 29:1-6.
5. How was Isaiah called to be a prophet? Isaiah 6:1-10.
6. By whom were great religious reforms instituted?
   II Chronicles 29:3-26, 30, 31:1-19.

7. How did the Assyrians defy Jerusalem, and what was the outcome? II Chronicles 32:1-23.
8. What great prophet had a conspicuous part in this victory over Assyria? II Kings 19.
9. Read Isaiah's account of Hezekiah's deliverance from the Assyrians. Isaiah 36-39.
10. What king's great wickedness sealed the doom of Judah? II Kings 21:1-16.
11. What was found that caused Josiah to institute drastic reforms? II Chron. 34:14-33, 35; II Kings 22, 23:1-28.
12. How did Josiah meet his death? II Chronicles 35:20-24; II Kings 23:29-30.
13. Quotation:
    "Then said I, here am I; send me." Isaiah 6:8.
14. Locate Babylon.

---

31. The Divided Kingdom—Judah (Concluded)

1. How did the Lord endeavor to save Judah?
   II Chronicles 36:11-20; Jeremiah 25:1-11.
2. What major prophet did God call during the reign of Josiah, the last good king? Jeremiah 1.
3. What was the cause of Jeremiah's lamentations?
   Lamentations 1:16.
4. What two minor prophets predicted Judah's fall?
   Zephaniah 1:1-4; Habakkuk 1:5-11.
5. Note the beautiful expression of trust amid disappointment and trial in Habakkuk 3:17-18. Compare with Daniel 3:16-18.
6. Who carried Judah captive and where?
   II Kings 24:10-20, 25:1-21.
7. Why did God permit the capture of Judah?
   II Kings 17; II Chronicles 30.
8. How long was Judah's captivity to last?
   Jeremiah 25:11-12, 29:10; II Chronicles 36:21.
9. Make a list of all the prophets God sent to warn Judah. (See the chart, page 49.)
10. Quotations:
    a. "His word was in mine heart as a burning fire shut up in my bones, and I was weary with forebearing, and I could not stay." Jeremiah 20:9.
    b. "The Lord is in His holy temple, let all the earth keep silence before Him." Habakkuk 2:20.

Statement. The Southern Kingdom, Judah, lasted 350 years, from 937 B.C. to 587 B.C., until it was conquered by Nebuchadnezzar, King of Babylonia, and many of its people taken away in captivity. Judah thus kept her national existence 135 years longer than Israel (Hurlbut).

V. The Period of Foreign Rule.

Introduction. This period extends from the fall of Jerusalem about 586 B.C. to the birth of Christ, covering a little less than 600 years. The Kingdom of Judah was resettled some fifty years later and became the basis of the Jewish nation of our Lord's time. The captivity, however, as predicted by Jeremiah and Daniel, had begun twenty years before in 606 B.C. when Daniel and other Hebrew princes were carried captive to Babylon. Our knowledge of this period is found in the books of Daniel and other prophets, in Esther, Ezra, Nehemiah, and in some of the Psalms.

The Northern Kingdom, Israel, fell with the capture of Samaria, 722 B.C., 135 years before the fall of Jerusalem. These people were taken captive into Assyria and are known as the "lost tribes of Israel."

32. Judah's Exile
(As found in Jeremiah, Ezekiel, and Daniel)

Jeremiah's ministry began before and continued during the exile of Judah, covering a period of about forty-two years. During these years he reproved the Jews for their sinful and idolatrous living and warned them of the impending judgments of God. Jeremiah believed that submission to the Babylonian king would prevent the complete destruction of Jerusalem, and he counseled them against resistance. Such counsel, however, led to accusations of treachery and finally to his imprisonment in the miry pit. He warned his people against seeking refuge in Egypt, but they disregarded this warning also and carried Jeremiah with them, against his will.

Make a list of the evils predicted against the people because of their sins. Jeremiah 19:7-9.

Ezekiel, the prophet, was born of a priestly family and educated in Judea. He was carried captive to Babylon eleven years before the fall of Jerusalem. That he was a leader among his fellow exiles is evidenced by the opening verses of Chapters 8, 14, and 20 where he speaks of the elders coming before him "to inquire of the Lord." Like Jeremiah he em-

phasized all the great teachings of Isaiah though in greatly
differing detail.

1. When and where did Ezekiel receive his call?
   Ezekiel 1:1-3.

2. To whom was Ezekiel sent? 2:1-5.

3. What promises of restoration were made to Judah?
   34:11-31.

4. In Chapter 33 note the prophet's charge (vs. 7-11) and
   the people's response (vs. 30-33).

Daniel, the last of the greater prophets, was carried captive
to Babylon in 606 B.C. He was educated with the Babylonian
princes for royal service. For seventy years or more his
righteousness, his wisdom, and his courage made him invaluable to Nebuchadnezzar and his successors, Belshazzar, Darius,
and Cyrus.

1. Why did Daniel, Shadrach, Meshach, and Abednego excel
   in wisdom and understanding? Daniel 1.

2. What was Nebuchadnezzar's dream and Daniel's interpretation of it? Chap. 2.

   (Note in this chapter the four great world empires which are
   seen: The Babylonian under Nebuchadnezzar, the Persian
   under Cyrus, the Grecian under Alexander the Great, and the
   Roman Empire.)

3. Why were Shadrach, Meshach, and Abednego thrown into
   the fiery furnace, and how were they delivered? Chap. 3.

4. Who interpreted the handwriting on the wall at Belshazzar's feast? 5:1-31.

5. Why was Daniel thrown into the lion's den, and how was
   he delivered? Chap. 6.

6. What foreign kings did Daniel serve? 1:1-2, 5:30-31,
   6:1-2.

7. Quotations:

   a. "Can the Ethiopian change his skin, or the leopard his
      spots?" Jeremiah 13:23.

   b. "Call unto me, and I will answer thee, and shew thee
      great and mighty things, which thou knowest not."
      Jeremiah 33:3.

   c "By the rivers of Babylon, there we sat down, yea, we
      wept when we remembered Zion." Psalm 137:1.

   d. "But Daniel purposed in his heart that he would not
      defile himself with the portion of the king's meat."
      Daniel 1:8.

   e. "Thou art weighed in the balances, and art found
      wanting." Daniel 5:27.

f. "And they that be wise shall shine as the brightness of the firmament; and they that turn many to righteousness as the stars forever and ever." Daniel 12:3.

---

33. Judah's Return from Exile
(As found in Ezra and Nehemiah)

The Return under Zerubbabel. Zerubbabel, whose name means *born in Babylon*, was a prince of the house of David and an ancestor of Christ. In 536 B.C. when Cyrus, the Persian king, issued decrees for the return of the Jews, Zerubbabel accompanied by Joshua, the high priest, led back to Jerusalem a band of 50,000 exiles. Under the leadership of these two men the Temple was rebuilt, and religious rites were restored.

1. In Isaiah 44:28 what king is foretold as rebuilding Jerusalem?
2. What liberal proclamation did Cyrus, the king of Persia, make to the Jews? Ezra 1:1-4.
3. What material contribution did he make toward the rebuilding of the Temple? Ezra 1:7-10.
4. Whom did the king appoint as governor of Judah? Haggai 1:14, 2:2; Ezra 3:8.
5. Who was the religious leader? Ezra 2:2, 3:2.
6. What two minor prophets began their work at this time and encouraged the people in the rebuilding of the Temple? Ezra 5:1, 6:14.
7. What caused the shouting and the praising mentioned in Ezra 3:10-13?
8. How did Zerubbabel's Temple compare with Solomon's in size, architectural splendor, and glory? Ezra 3:12, 6:3; Haggai 2:3-9. (See Question 6, Lesson 25.)
9. On what eminence in the city of Jerusalem were both Temples built? Who chose this site? II Samuel 24:18; I Chronicles 21:18-30, 22:1; II Chronicles 3:1.
10: Quotations:
    a. "For we are bondmen; yet our God hath not forsaken us in our bondage, but hath extended mercy unto us." Ezra 9:9.
    b. "They that sow in tears shall reap in joy." Psalm 126:5.

The Return under Ezra. Ezra was a scribe and an interpreter of the Law of Moses. It is generally believed that he

contributed much to the arrangement of the Old Testament
Canon and that he was founder of the synagogue. In 458 B.C.,
seventy-eight years after the first return, he obtained leave
from Artaxerxes to go to Jerusalem and take with him a com-
pany of Israelites. His first step was to enforce a separation
upon all Jews who had married foreign wives. Nothing more
is said about him until thirteen years later when he assisted
Nehemiah in instituting religious reforms.

1. To which of the twelve tribes did Ezra belong?
    Ezra 7:1-5.
2. What was his preparation as a scribe and as an inter-
    preter? Ezra 7:10, 25.
3. Read Ezra 7:11-26 noting King Artaxerxes' admiration
    for Ezra, his faith in Jehovah, and his respect for the
    laws of Jehovah.
4. Whom did Ezra insist upon taking with him and why?
    Ezra 8:15-17.
5. Why was he displeased with the first group that had
    returned under Zerubbabel? Ezra 9:1-2.
6. What prophet was contemporary with Ezra and Nehemiah
    in the reforms of Judah? Malachi 1:6-9, 2:17.
7. What is taught in Malachi 3:10? How does this compare
    with the teaching found in I Corinthians 16:2?

---

34. Judah's Return from Exile (Concluded)

The Return under Nehemiah. Nehemiah was a loyal Jewish
exile who had become cupbearer to the Persian king. Thirteen
years after Ezra's return, Nehemiah obtained permission from
Artaxerxes to go to Jerusalem to rebuild the walls which were
still in ruins. He showed such wisdom in arousing the people
to action, in directing the reconstruction, and in coping with
the opposition that arose on every hand, and in setting up
religious reforms that he may well be called one of the great
statesmen of Old Testament times, a masterful man of God.

1. What did Nehemiah learn from his relatives concerning
    the state of affairs in Jerusalem? Neh. 1:2-3.
2. Nehemiah's prayer indicates what about his understand-
    ing of God's promises and his faith in them? Neh.
    1:5-11.
3. How did the king learn of Nehemiah's desires and why
    did he grant them? Neh. 2:1-8.
4. What preparation did he make for his work?
    Neh. 2:11-16.

5. List the different kinds of opposition Nehemiah had to deal with, and note in each instance how he through confidence in God overcame each hindrance. Neh. 4:1, 7-8, 10, 5:1-10, 6:2, 6:7-13.

6. Give an example of his unselfishness. Neh. 5:14-19.

7. Who assisted him in establishing religious reforms? Neh. 8:1.

8. How did the Jews show their reverence for the Word of God? Neh. 8:3-6.

9. How was the completion of the wall celebrated? Neh. 12:27-43.

10. What reforms were wrought by Nehemiah on his second visit? Neh. 13:4-31.

11. Quotations:
   a. "So built we the wall . . . : for the people had a mind to work." Nehemiah 4:6.
   b. "And the king granted me, according to the good hand of my God upon me." Nehemiah 2:8.

35. Esther

Introduction. The Book of Esther is based upon a Jewish persecution which occurred about 485 B.C. The heroine of the story is Esther, the Queen of Ahasuerus, the Persian ruler. She is an exiled Jewish maiden of rare beauty, whose patriotic zeal is so tempered with tact and sound judgment that her appeal to the King in behalf of her people is heard, and she saves them from the ban of extermination. While the name of God is not mentioned in the story, the reader feels, as Mordecai does, that Providence has lifted Esther to this position "for such a time as this." (Esther 4:13-14.)

NOTE: Chronologically this lesson should come between *The Return under Zerubbabel and The Return under Ezra*, but it has been placed here in order to preserve the continuity of thought in Lesson 33.

1. What was the extent of the Persian ruler's kingdom? Esther 1:1.

2. The Feast of Ahasuerus continued how many months? 1:4.

3. How did the men and the women of the royal house spend the last seven days of the feast? 1:5-9.

4. Why was Queen Vashti dethroned? 1:10-22.

5. Who was chosen to fill her place? Chap. 2.

6. Who was Esther's foster father? Of what tribe was he?
   2:5-7.
7. What conspiracy did Mordecai disclose? 2:19-23.
8. Why was Mordecai in disfavor with Haman, the king's
   grand vizier? 3:1-5.
9. What was the decree of Haman? 3:6-15.
10. How did Esther risk her life to save her people?
   Chaps. 4 and 5.
11. Why and how was Mordecai honored? 6:1-11.
12. How was Haman's plot revealed to the king? 7:1-6.
13. What was Haman's punishment? 7:9-10.
14. How were the Jews saved? Chaps. 8 and 9.
15. What feast commemorates the preservation of the Jews
   from massacre? 9:20-28.
16. Quotations:
   a. "Who knoweth whether thou art come to the kingdom
      for such a time as this?" 4:14.
   b. "If I perish, I perish." 4:16.

NOTE: Esther 8:9 is the longest verse in the Bible.
Psalm 119 is the longest chapter in the Bible.

36. Prophets

Introduction. About one-fourth of the Old Testament is
composed of the books known as the "Prophets." These books
bear the names of their human authors and contain many
practical exhortations as well as prophecies. It will be remembered that besides these whose prophetic writings are in the
Bible there were other prophets in Israel's history such as
Moses, Deborah, Samuel, Nathan, Elijah, and Elisha. It is
also true that some prophecy is found in nearly every book of
the Bible. One of the strongest evidences of the Bible's Divine
origin is the fact of fulfilled prophecy.

Many prophecies were fulfilled in the course of history
before Christ (e.g., Ezekiel 26:7-14); many others were fulfilled in Christ and the New Testament; while still others await
fulfillment (e.g., Micah 4:1-4).

The prophets are usually divided into two groups, (1) The
Major Prophets: Isaiah, Jeremiah (and Lamentations), Ezekiel, and Daniel. (2) The Minor Prophets: the remaining
twelve—Hosea through Malachi. This classification is based
on the amount of material in the books.

By such phrases as "Thus saith the Lord," "The word of the Lord came unto the prophet," it is evident that the prophet considered his message to be direct from God. These messages usually include rebuke of sin and warning of impending judgment, as well as predictions and promises of comfort and blessing. Jonah and Nahum are addressed to Nineveh and Obadiah to Edom. All the others are primarily to Judah and Israel.

Another classification which is suitable for this study may be made in relation to the captivity or "exile" of Judah: (1) Pre-exilic, (2) Exilic, and (3) Post-exilic. The chart on page 49, will prove helpful. See, also, the *Introduction* to the *Monarchic Period*, second paragraph, page 30.

1. Define the term, *prophet*. How did the *prophets* differ from the *priests?* (See page 30.)
2. Who was the first to be called a prophet? (See Note,¹ page 30.)
3. The first school of prophets was founded by whom? (See *Introduction* to Lesson 20.)
4. Books of prophecy comprise how much of the Old Testament?
5. What is the strongest evidence of the Bible's divine origin?
6. Prophets are usually divided into what two groups? Upon what is this classification based?
7. Name the prophets in each of these two groups. See page 49.
8. Explain the meaning of the terms, *pre-exilic, exilic,* and *post-exilic* as applied to the prophets.
9. Whose prophetic ministry extended over two periods, pre-exilic and exilic?
10. Who is generally considered the greatest of the prophets and why?
11. Quotations:
    a. "For the prophecy came not in old time by the will of man: but holy men of God spake as they were moved by the Holy Ghost." II Peter 1:21. (Peter's explanation of the origin of the Bible.)
    b. "The Lord hath given me the tongue of the learned, that I should know how to speak a word in season to him that is weary." Isaiah 50:4. (Isaiah speaks of his divine inspiration.)
    c. "The spirit of the Lord spake by me, and His word was in my tongue." II Samuel 23:2. (David speaks of his divine inspiration.)

37. Prophecies Concerning the Coming of Christ

Messianic prophecy permeates the Old Testament, beginning with Genesis 3:15 and continuing to Malachi 3:1.

Pre-Exilic Prophecy.

Joel, whose name means *Jehovah God,* was one of the earliest prophets sent to Judah. Some believe that he prophesied as early as 850 B.C., making him contemporaneous with Elijah and Elisha. He exhorted Judah to repentance, predicting a plague of locusts, a severe drought, and invasions of the enemy. He gave assurance that God would hear the prayer of the penitent, deliver them from evil, and bless them with plenty. Besides these material blessings there was a promise of a great spiritual awakening. On the Day of Pentecost about 880 years later, the Apostle Peter declared, "This is that which was spoken by the prophet Joel." Acts 2:16.

How is the promise of Joel 2:28-32 related to the Day of Pentecost? Acts 2:16-21.

Isaiah (756-701 B.C.), the greatest of all the prophets, is quoted more than any other in the New Testament. No other prophet has so much to say about the Messiah.

NOTE: Other facts in the life of Isaiah may be found in Lesson 30.

1. Read the following prophecies concerning the coming of the Messiah: Isaiah 7:14, 9:6-7, 11:1-5, 42:1-7, Chap. 53.
2. Read what Isaiah says about the future glories of the Messiah's kingdom. 2:2-5, 11:6-9, Chap. 35.
3. What names are given to the coming Messiah? 9:6.
4. Compare Isaiah 61:1-2 with Luke 4:16-19.

Micah, a Judean peasant, was a contemporary of Isaiah. Since he predicted the fall of Samaria (Micah 1:6), he must have begun his ministry long before 722 B.C. His message was a plea against social injustice. He centered his attacks upon the capitals of the two kingdoms where he thought the existing evils were the most concentrated. In his long look into the future he saw Jerusalem triumphant as the capital of the Messianic Kingdom and the little town of Bethlehem chosen "among the thousands of Judah."

1. What is Micah's picture of world peace in 4:4-8?
2. What was the honor to be conferred upon Bethlehem? 5:2.
3. Under what circumstances was Micah 5:2 quoted in Matthew 2:5-7?

(Arranged in probable chronological order)

Prophet	Rank	Probable Date	To Whom Sent	Rulers on the Throne	Probable Contemporaneous Prophets
Elijah	Oral	876-850 B.C.	Israel	Ahab	Joel
Elisha	Oral	855-797 B.C.	Israel	Ahaziah, Jehoram, Jehu, Johoahaz	Joel
Joel	Minor	850 B.C.	Judah	Jehoram	Elijah, Elisha
Obadiah	Minor	830 B.C.	Edom	Jehoash	Elisha
Micah	Minor	756-710 B.C.	Judah, Israel	Jotham, Ahaz, Hezekiah	Isaiah, Hosea, Amos, Jonah
Isaiah	Major	756-701 B.C.	Judah	Uzziah, Jotham, Ahaz, Hezekiah	Hosea, Amos, Jonah, Micah
Jonah	Minor	750 B.C.	Nineveh	Jeroboam II	Isaiah, Hosea, Amos, Micah
Amos	Minor	750 B.C.	Israel	Uzziah and Jeroboam II	Isaiah, Hosea, Jonah, Micah
Hosea	Minor	750-705 B.C.	Israel, Judah	Jeroboam II and all kings to the fall of Samaria	Isaiah, Amos, Jonah, Micah

722 B.C. The Fall of Samaria

Prophet	Rank	Probable Date	To Whom Sent	Rulers on the Throne	Probable Contemporaneous Prophets
Nahum	Minor	640 B.C.	Nineveh	Amon and Josiah	None
Jeremiah	Major	627-577 B.C.	Judah	Josiah, Jehoiakim, Zedekiah	Ezekiel, Daniel, Habakkuk, and Zephaniah
Habakkuk	Minor	600? B.C.	Judah	Jehoiakim, Jehoiachin, Zedekiah	Jeremiah, Daniel
Zephaniah	Minor	625 B.C.	Judah	Josiah	Jeremiah, Ezekiel

606 B.C. First Babylonian Captivity

Prophet	Rank	Probable Date	To Whom Sent	Rulers on the Throne	Probable Contemporaneous Prophets
Daniel	Major	606-536 B.C.	Judah, Babylon, Persia	Zedekiah, Nebuchadnezzar, Belshazzar, Darius, Cyrus	Jeremiah, Ezekiel, Habakkuk, and Zephaniah
Ezekiel	Major	594-573 B.C.	Judah	Jehoakim, Zedekiah	Jeremiah, Daniel

587 B.C. The Fall of Jerusalem
537 B.C. Return of Judah from Exile

Prophet	Rank	Probable Date	To Whom Sent	Rulers on the Throne	Probable Contemporaneous Prophets
Haggai	Minor	520 B.C.	Judah	Persian Kings	Zachariah
Zechariah	Minor	520 B.C.	Judah	Persian Kings	Haggai
Malachi	Minor	450 B.C.	Judah	Persian Kings	None

(This chart is for reference only. Pupils are not expected to know the details given.)

Habakkuk is one of the minor prophets about whose life little is known. Many, however, believe that he prophesied at the same time Jeremiah did. His message opens with a dialogue between himself and God. The subject is the injustices which the Hebrews will have to suffer from the Chaldean invasion, and he dared to complain about it. God convinces him that these foreign people are instruments in his divine plan, and when the prophet ascends his "watchtower" which lifts him spiritually, he is in closer communion with God and sees that the world conqueror will be the Lord himself.

What does Habakkuk say about the growth of the Kingdom? 2:14.

Exilic Prophecy.

Jeremiah's ministry began before the Captivity and continued during the Exile (627-577 B.C.). See page 41.

What are the promises found in Jeremiah 23:5-6 and 31:31-34? In 23:6 what does Jeremiah say Jesus shall be called?

Daniel, who prophesied from 606 to 536 B. C., is called the prophet of "the Times of the Gentiles." See page 42.

What is to be the final empire as pictured in Daniel 2:44-45?

Ezekiel, one of the four great prophets of Israel, ministered to his exiled people from 592-570 B.C., giving them a message of hopefulness.

1. In Ezekiel 17:22-24 what do the mighty tree and the tender twig symbolize? Read Daniel 2:34.
2. In 34:23-24 and 37:24 the shepherd and prince is to possess the traditional qualities of whom? Read Psalm 23:1.

Post-Exilic Prophecy.

Haggai, who began his prophetic work about 520 B.C., was among those who returned from captivity under Zerubbabel.

What does Haggai prophesy in 2:7-9?

Zechariah was probably among those who returned from captivity under Zerubbabel in 535 B.C. He called the people to repentance and eight visions followed. These were given with the hope of encouraging the people to rebuild the Temple.

1. What is the prediction in Zechariah 9:9?

2. What familiar New Testament situation is indicated by Zechariah 11:12-13 and 13:6-7?

Malachi prophesied about three hundred years after Isaiah and about one hundred years after Zechariah. He is generally believed to have been a contemporary of Ezra and Nehemiah. He preached against the same evils with which they had to contend. Malachi concluded his message with an exhortation to remember the Law of Moses, and in his last two verses he predicted the coming of John the Baptist, the forerunner of Christ.

What New Testament character fulfills Malachi 3:1 and 4:5-6?

Quotations:

1. "I will pour out my spirit upon all flesh; and your sons and your daughters shall prophesy, your old men shall dream dreams, and your young men shall see visions." Joel 2:28.

2. "For unto us a child is born, unto us a son is given: and the government shall be upon his shoulder: and his name shall be called Wonderful, Counsellor, The mighty God, The everlasting Father, The Prince of Peace." Isaiah 9:6.

3. "And they shall beat their swords into plowshares, and their spears into pruning hooks." Isaiah 2:4.

4. "For the earth shall be filled with the knowledge of the glory of the Lord, as the waters cover the sea." Hab. 2:14.

5. "But they shall sit every man under his vine and under his fig tree; and none shall make them afraid." Micah 4:4.

6. "Behold, the days come, saith the Lord, that I will raise unto David a righteous Branch, and a King shall reign and prosper, and shall execute judgment and justice in the earth." Jeremiah 23:5.

7. "Not by might, nor by power, but by my spirit, saith the Lord of hosts." Zachariah 4:6.

8. "Behold, I will send my messenger, and he shall prepare the way before me." Malachi 3:1.

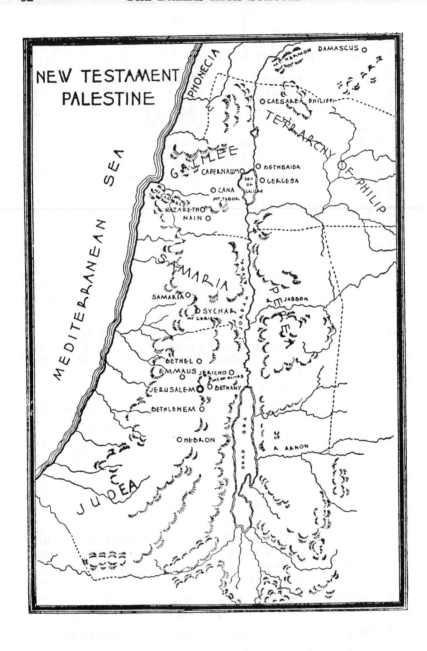

38. John the Baptist, the Forerunner of Christ

Introduction. For centuries God had been sending forerunners to prepare the way for the advent of his Son. Not only had he sent patriarchs, psalmists, poets, and prophets, but history gives evidence of his having made universal preparation.

At the birth of Christ conditions were particularly suitable for the spread of a new faith. The world was under the rule of the Roman Empire. The Greek language was universally used and understood. Transportation from place to place in the Empire was comparatively swift and sure, by boat, well-made roads, and everywhere travelers were under the protection of a trained soldiery. The Jewish people, finding it impossible to regain their complete national independence, had turned their attention to matters of religious controversy and there was a general feeling of expectancy among the devout Jews that God would visit and deliver his people.

Many centuries had elapsed since Isaiah had exhorted the children of Israel. " . . . . to prepare the way of the Lord, make straight in the desert a highway for our God." At least four centuries had passed since Malachi in an effort to give hope to the returned exiles had prophesied, "Behold, I will send my messenger, and he shall prepare the way before me." This prophecy found its fulfillment in John the Baptist, who made his appearance only six months before the advent of the Messiah.

1. What is the first indication in the Bible that Jesus would come? See Lessons 2 and 37.

2. Read the following Old Testament prophecies concerning the coming of John the Baptist: Isaiah 40:3; Malachi 3:1, 2; 4:5, 6. Compare these prophecies with the following statements found in the New Testament: John 1:22, 23; Mark 1:1-7; Matthew 11:9-11, 14-15.

3. Who were the parents of John the Baptist, and what is said about their righteousness? Luke 1:5-25.

4. Summarize the story of his birth. Luke 1:57-66.

5. What does Zacharias prophesy concerning his son? Luke 1:67-79.

6. Where did John live until he began to preach? Luke 1:80.

7. Describe his dress and manner of living. Matthew 3:4.

8. Explain the meaning of the term, *forerunner*. Why was John called a forerunner of Jesus? Matthew 3:3.

9. What was his message? Matthew 3:2.

10. What did he testify concerning the Messiah, and how did he compare himself to Jesus? Mark 1:7; John 1:23.

11. Quotations:

    a. "There cometh one mightier than I after me, the latchet of whose shoes I am not worthy to stoop down and unloose." Mark 1:7.

    b. "I am the voice of one crying in the wilderness, Make straight the way of the Lord." John 1:23.

39. Review Lesson

Systematic reviews should be made during the progress of the course, but there is also need for a careful general review at the conclusion of the course. If pupils feel that they have a good knowledge of the course and an understanding of just what is expected of them on the final examination, they will undertake the examination with assurance and confidence. The nature and scope of the final examination is well illustrated in the copy of final examination questions, pp. 79-85. These questions should be studied carefully, and the different types of questions observed. Close attention should be given to "Minimum Requirements," pp. x-xi. The articles in the Appendix are not required lesson materials, but pupils should read these articles at appropriate times during the progress of the course and be able to answer the questions at the end of each article. Finally, pupils should be asked to summarize under a few headings the chief benefits they have received from the course.

Questions

1. Regulations governing the course
    a. Who may take the Old Testament Course?
    b. What is said about attendance? How must absences be made up?

   c. Who may take the final examination?

   d. What is the minimum passing grade?

   e. What examination grade is necessary for eligibility in certain contests and awards?

2. Minimum requirements
   a. Note carefully the items in each of the twelve divisions.
   b. Be able to quote accurately all required memory work (p. 75).

3. Final examination
   a. Who gives the final examination? When and where is it given?
   b. Study carefully the copy of final examination questions included in your text (p. 79). Note the different types of questions.
   c. Try your hand at making out a set of final examination questions.

4. Value of course
   a. Write under a few headings the chief benefits you have received from this course.
   b. Try to summarize a few of the great lessons God revealed to the Hebrews in his dealings with them.

   NOTE: Read "Bible History, a History of Redemption" by T. M. Dalton, p. 70, optional.

There are no songs comparable to the songs of Zion, no orations equal to those of the prophets, and no politics like those which the Scriptures teach.

JOHN MILTON.

We search the world for truth: we cull
The good, the pure, the beautiful,
From graven stone and written scroll,
From old flower fields of the soul;
And, weary seekers of the best,
We come back laden from our quest,
To find that all the sages said
Is in the book our mothers read.

WHITTIER.

APPENDIX

SELECTED BIBLIOGRAPHY

ARCHAEOLOGY

Barton, George A. *Archaeology of the Bible*, American Sunday School Union (3.50).

Kinnemon, J. O. *Diggers for Facts*, Destiny Publishing Co., 1941.

Marston, Sir Chas. *New Bible Evidence*, Revell, 1933 (2.50).

Muir, J. C. *His Truth Endureth*, National Pub. Co., 1937 (2.50). (O. T.)

Muir, J. C. *The Spade and the Scriptures*. Broadway Press ($1.00). (A study course.)

Price, Ira M. *The Monuments of the Old Testament*, Judson Press, 1924 ($2.50).

Prescott, W. W. *The Spade and the Bible*. Revell ($2.50.)

Rimmer, Harry. *Dead Men Tell Tales*. Eerdman Publishing Co., 1939 ($2.50).

ATLAS

Browne, Lewis. *The Graphic Bible*. Macmillan ($1.00), 1942.

Hurlbut, J. L. *Bible Atlas*. Rand McNally, 1938 ($3.50).

BACKGROUNDS

Adams, J. McKee. *Biblical Backgrounds*. Boardman Press, 1934 ($3.75).

Baike, James. *Lands and Peoples of the Bible*. Macmillan ($1.75).

Harrell, C. J. *The Bible: Its Origin and Growth*. Cokesbury, 1926 ($1.00).

Morton, H. V. *Through the Land of the Bible*. Halcyon House ($1.79).

Soares, Theo. G. *The Origins of the Bible*. Harpers, 1941 ($2.50).

COMMENTARY

Dummelow, J. R. *One Volume Bible Commentary*. Macmillan, 1943 ($3.00).

Eislen-Lewis-Downey. *Abingdon Bible Commentary*. Abingdon Press, 1929 ($5.00).

Irwin, C. H. *The International Bible Commentary*. Winston, 1928 ($2.50).

Tidwell, J. B. *The Bible Book by Book*. Ederman Publishing Co. ($1.75).

CONCORDANCE

Cruden, Alexander. *A Complete Concordance.* Winston ($2.00).

Joy, Charles R. *Harper's Topical Concordance.* Harper, 1940 ($3.95).

Walker, J. B. R. *The Comprehensive Concordance to the Holy Scriptures.* Macmillan, 1941 ($3.00).

DICTIONARY

Graebner, Theodore. *Dictionary of Bible Topics.* Zondervan Publishing House, Grand Rapids, Mich., 1943 ($2.00).

Hastings, James. *Dictionary of the Bible.* Scribners, 1937 ($8.00). (Standard.)

Peloubet. *Bible Dictionary.* Winston, 1925 ($2.50).

Smith, William. *Bible Dictionary.* Winston, 1938 ($2.25).

GENERAL

Dalton, T. M. *A Comprehensive Bible Study Course.* Mathis Van Nort Co., 1940 ($1.50).

Egermeir, Elsie E. *The Story of the Bible.* Warner Press, 1939 ($2.50).

Goodspeed, Edgar J. *Story of the Old Testament.* University of Chicago Press ($1.00).

Goodspeed-Smith. *American Translation of the Bible.* University of Chicago Press ($2.00).

Gray, J. M. *Synthetic Bible Studies.* Revell ($2.25).

Josephus. *Antiquities of the Bible.* Winston ($2.50).

Hurlbut, J. L. *The Story of the Bible.* Winston ($2.00).

Morgan, G. C. *Studies of the Minor Prophets.* Revell ($1.25).

Morton, H. V. *Women of the Bible.* Dodd Mead & Co., 1941 ($2.00).

Terrell, Ada Thurman. *An Outline Course in Bible Study.* Revell, 1927 ($1.50).

The Universal Jewish Encyclopedia. Universal Jewish Encyclopedia Inc., 1939, New York.

(NOTE: Prices may vary as of current date.)

Try to comprehend as much as possible of this book with your mind, and accept the rest on faith, and you will live and die a better man.

ABRAHAM LINCOLN.

THE LAND AND THE BOOK*

By WILLIAM NEHEMIAH WIGGINS,
*For twenty-five years General Superintendent
of Texas Sunday School Association*

Someone said, "The Land is the fifth Gospel." It is absolutely impossible to understand fully the meaning of the language used in the Bible without having a comprehensive knowledge of the geography of the land and the customs and manners of the people which prevailed when the Bible was written.

The following brief paragraphs have been compiled with the hope that they may be helpful to teachers of Bible classes, particularly to the less experienced teacher. We have quoted very liberally from "The Teaching Values of the Old Testament," by Drs. W. W. Moore and Edward Mack, which has been fully verified by the writer, in almost every detail, while he personally visited and studied the land in connection with the World Sunday School Convention at Jerusalem in 1904.

The Palestinian Atmosphere of the Bible. "Like other books, the Bible has had a home, a birthplace; but beyond all other examples, this birthplace has given color and form to its language." The phraseology and imagery of the Bible reflect in a remarkable degree the character of the country in which it was written and the customs of the people among whom it arose. We must learn the land and the life of ancient Israel if we would apprehend the whole setting of revealed truth and appreciate the force of a multitude of metaphors and allusions which otherwise would have no meaning.

The Land and the Redemptive Purpose of God. Not only is it essential to study Palestine for an intelligent appreciation of Biblical forms and statements of surface facts of Biblical history, but it is vital to a full understanding of the inner relations of those facts to each other as parts of one divine purpose and stages in one divine revelation, unfolded gradually through hundreds of years and culminating in a universal religion.

The Land of Promise was preconfigured to its history. It was through the characteristics of the country that God effected fulfillment of the promise of Abraham, that in his seed should all the nations of the earth be blessed. By its location and structure it was adapted, as no other country on

---

*NOTE: To Drs. W. W. Moore and Edward Mack in *Teaching Values* of Old Testament, we are indebted for much of the descriptions contained in this outline on "The Land and the Book." The present article is an abridgment of an earlier treatment prepared by Mr. Wiggins.

earth, to God's purpose of preparing a pure religion through centuries of separation and then of publishing that religion to the whole world. For the accomplishment of these ends, three things seemed necessary:

1. A single nation had to be chosen as the special depository of divine truth. This nation had to be *separated* from all other nations in order that this truth might be preserved and developed in its purity. This isolation of Israel was secured by natural barriers of desert, river, sea, and mountain.

2. This nation had to be set in the *center* of the world so that when "the fullness of time was come," the saving truth which it possessed might be easily proclaimed to all mankind. Palestine was central. It was the focal point of the ancient world. It commanded access to three great continents—Europe, Asia, and Africa. Palestine stood in the midst of the nations of antiquity. It was therefore fitted, as no other land was, to be the radiating center of a universal relgion.

3. The book which contained this revelation had to be a *universal* book. It could not be local or sectional. It must possess such a range of imagery and style as would make it easily understood by men of every race in every land. The Record of the Truth thus prepared had to be such as would fit it for world-wide dissemination. It must speak to the universal heart of man by its essential truth. It must have characteristics of form adapted to the ready understanding of men of all lands.

The structure of Palestine. Palestine could not have been a mere accident in God's creation. The structure of Palestine preeminently fitted it to produce such a book as the Bible. It is a very small country, ranging from 25 to 75 miles in width, and about 140 miles in length. Yet in this small strip we have extraordinary differences of elevation and climate, with snow on Mount Hermon and torrid heat at Jericho. Mount Hermon has an elevation of 9,200 feet above the Mediterranean, and the Dead Sea is 1,292 feet below the Mediterranean. This great variation in topography accounts for the amazing variety of animal and vegetable life, representing widely separated zones and making it a sort of epitome of the whole earth. "Accordingly, the illustrations drawn from nature, with which the Bible abounds, are suited to all climes and understood by all men."

The Land's Natural Divisions. Palestine consists of four strips of territory, running parallel to each other north and south, with two elevations and two depressions alternating. A narrow plain skirts the Mediterranean. Next to this is a tumbled and broken ridge rising to an altitude of 3,000 feet. Then comes the extraordinary depressions through which flows the River Jordan; and after this, the elevated tablelands lying between the Jordan and the Eastern Desert.

The Mediterranean Plain a Highway. This narrow Mediterranean plain, level or gently undulating, open at both ends, was the bridge between Asia and Africa. It was traversed by highways along which the caravans and armies of two continents passed to and fro. Here we find the real contribution of Israel to history. By the Trunk Road through this plain, the Philistines came up to the overthrow of Saul at Mount Gilboa. Along this road the Jews saw the armies of Tiglah-Pileser, Shalmaneser, Saragon, Sennacherib, Pharaoh-Necho, and Nebuchadnezzar pass. It was the world's highway.

The most striking feature of the coast line is that it had no good harbor. The Hebrews had no word for harbor because they had no need for the name. To them the sea was a barrier and not a highway. That long line of sand, unbroken by any deep indentation, cut Israel off almost entirely from water communication with the western world. *Seclusion* is the dominant note in the *Old Testament.* *Expansion* is the dominant note in the *New Testament.* When God's time came He raised a man, who was unconsciously His instrument for the breaking of a gateway through which the Gospel should go forth to the west. Herod the Great, for the first time in history, built a real harbor for Palestine at Caesarea. Thence the Great Apostle to the Gentiles went forth with the Gospel to the Western World.

The Plain of Esdraelon a Highway and Battlefield. Esdraelon is the great triangular plain which breaks the continuity of the Central Ridge and affords clear passage from the coast to the Jordan. Through this plain the marauding Bedouin passed from the East. The armies of the great empires passed this way; hence, the plain's history as a great battlefield. Isa. 19:23.

Samaria Easy of Access. The gentle ridges of the west offer an easy access from the coast. Interspersed among the mountains in the center are plains, meadows, and spacious vales; hence the land was easy for chariots. "All the long drives of the Old Testament are in Samaria." One result was frequent invasions. Its connection with Eastern Palestine has existed from the earliest times to the present day. The easy access the easy passes, and numerous fords of the Jordan here, are in sharp contrast with the separation of Judea from the East, because of the steep chasm and the few and dangerous fords farther south. Through the accessibility of Samaria, the "surrounding paganism poured into her ample life." Samaria suffered many changes of rulers. The Northern Kingdom had nine dynasties. The Southern Kingdom had only one dynasty. The Northern Kingdom fell more than a hundred years before the Southern. In short, as Smith says, Samaria was more forward to attract than Judea, but less able to retain.

Spiritual Supremacy of Judea. Judea was the heart of the Land of Palestine, the seat of Israel's one enduring dynasty, the site of her Temple, and the platform of all her chief prophets. Isolated, unattractive, provincial, conservative, she held the world off longest. Study carefully the borders and bulwarks of this stony plateau. The most accessible frontier was on the north, and here accordingly many battles were fought. Judea was a stronghold, not impregnable, but very difficult to take. (It is interesting to study the direction from which General Allenby of the Allies came to capture Jerusalem during the World War.) Outstanding features of the province are its pastoral character, says Smith, and its vine culture, and its natural unfitness for the growth of a large city. Aloof, waterless, on the road to nowhere, yet here arose the city which has taught the world civil justice, has given through the Cross eternal salvation, and has given her name to the ideal city hoped for—the New Jerusalem.

The Jordan Valley a Barrier. The lower Jordan is thought of as a border and a barrier. The name is nearly always governed by a preposition, "unto," "over," "across." A jungle along its bank, it is a symbol of trouble and danger. Study the miraculous way Israel crossed the Jordan here.

The Eastern Range. The Eastern Highlands are generally well-watered and fertile; but being separated from the body of the nation by the gorge of the Jordan, had comparatively small influence on the course of history.

The Manners and Customs of the People. The imagery of scripture, since it is drawn from natural scenery, is consequently readily understood in all parts of the world. Not so with the customs and manners of the people. The Old Testament is an Oriental book, as is the New very largely. The life the Bible describes belongs to the East and is widely different from the life in the West. Nearly every feature of it is foreign to our experience, and it undergoes very little change from age to age.

In recent times capitalists and settlers from without, have come in and introduced many modern features, such as railroads, telegraph lines, printing presses, automobiles, airplanes, hotels, etc. Still all these have to this day had very little or practically no effect on the patriarchal usages of the body of the people.

QUESTIONS

1. Why is a knowledge of the geography of Palestine necessary in a Bible study course?
2. Give three geographic reasons that make Palestine suitable for the giving of the Bible.
3. What is the size of Palestine?
4. Give the two extremes of altitude in Palestine.
5. Name the main geographic divisions of the land.
6. What is meant by the terms "the highway of the nations" and "the battlefield of the nations?"
7. Give at least three geographic reasons that caused Samaria's downfall before Jerusalem's.

IMPORTANT PEOPLES OF BIBLE TIMES

The study of the Bible will be made easier and more interesting if a knowledge of the principal peoples of Biblical times is gained in advance of or in connection with the study of the Bible. The following brief summary should be helpful in this connection:

1. *The Hebrews.* These were the central people of the Old Testament. They are designated by three names: (1) Hebrews, after Abram (Abraham) called the "Hebrew" or "crosser," presumably because he crossed over Mesopotamia to Canaan; (2) Israelites, after Jacob, who was also called "Israel"; (3) Jews, a term used after the Exile, and having reference to the tribe of Judah or Judea, their home. These peoples were members of the Semitic family, being descendants of Shem, who was one of the sons of Noah. They belonged to the Semitic race, as did the Assyrians and Babylonians. About 2,000 B.C. Abraham moved out of an old center called Chaldea to Canaan (Palestine) to become the father of the Hebrew nation, "the chosen people of God."

2. *Babylonians and Assyrians.* These peoples inhabited the Tigris-Euphrates valley where they built the great capital cities of Babylon and Nineveh, and developed one of the greatest of ancient civilizations. In 722 B.C. the Assyrians conquered Samaria, the northern kingdom of Israel, and carried the inhabitants into captivity. The southern kingdom of Judah was finally captured by Nebuchadnezzar in 586 B.C. Hammurabi, the great ruler of Babylon, was a contemporary

of Abraham and the author of the code which bears his name. He is referred to in the Bible as Amraphel (Gen. 14:9). The Babylonians and Assyrians, while largely of the same racial stock as the Hebrews, were great idolaters and polytheists.

Babylon was later captured by Cyrus, who established the Medo-Persian Empire and permitted many Jews to return to their own land and partially re-establish their national life.

3. *Egyptians.* Egypt, which lies to the south of Canaan, built up a great civilization. The Egyptians became strong rivals of the eastern nations and contended with them for control of Palestine, which because of its intermediate position, was commercially important. For a long time Egypt was friendly to the Hebrews and for 400 years was their chief home. When the government of Egypt became oppressive to the Hebrews, they were led out under the guidance of Moses.

4. *The Canaanites and Other Peoples.* Other peoples which deserve mention are the Syrians, who lived to the northeast of Palestine; the Phoenicians, to the northwest; the Philistines, to the southwest; and, besides the Canaanites, various other small groups, including the Edomites, Ammonites, Amalekites, etc.

5. *Greeks and Romans.* Before and during the New Testament times Greek and Roman culture and language played an important part. The Roman government gained control of Palestine about 45 B.C. and held this control throughout the New Testament period.

QUESTIONS

1. By what other names are the Hebrews known?
2. What was Hammurabi?
3. In what way are Abram and Hammurabi related?
4. Name five important peoples who lived in or adjacent to Palestine.

All that I have taught of art, everything that I have written, every greatness that there has been in any thought of mine, whatever I have done in my life, has been simply due to the fact that when I was a child my mother daily read to me a portion of the Bible, and daily made me learn a part of it by heart.
JOHN RUSKIN.

LANGUAGE AND MANUSCRIPTS
OF THE BIBLE*

By Dr. GLENN L. SNEED,
Former Pastor of Trinity Presbyterian Church, Dallas

1. *Name.* The name Bible is derived from the Greek word *Biblos*, meaning "Book" or "The Book." The term *biblos* is itself said to be derived from *byblos*, the inner bark of the papyrus reed on which early writings were inscribed. Well may the Bible be called "the Book." It is the best seller in all of the greatest book stores in the world and is the most widely quoted book in the world's best literature.

2. *Language.* Most of the Old Testament is written in the Hebrew language. A number of small portions (Jer. 10:11; Dan. 2:4-7:28; Ezra 4:8-6:18, 7:12-26) and a few scattered words are written in a tongue called "Aramaic," formerly known as "Chaldee." For centuries Aramaic was the language of the people north of Palestine (northern Syria, western Mesopotamia, and southeastern Asia Minor). The New Testament was written not in classical Greek, nor even in the literary Greek of New Testament times, but in the common Greek language of everyday life.

3. *Hand Writing.* The earliest copies that we have of the Bible are written in uncial letters; that is, capital letters. There were no spaces between the words and in the case of the Hebrew the vowels had to be supplied by the reader. The later translations were written in the cursive or running hand.

4. *Original Manuscripts.* Everything written on perishable material such as papyrus and skin is always in great danger of being lost or destroyed. Men of old realized this fact and in order to preserve the sacred writings, and at the same time give copies to more people, they laboriously transcribed them again and again. There were numerous copies other than the original in existence. Consequently from these copies of the original manuscripts others were made. Had it not been for this, the Bible would not be known to us, for not a single copy of an original manuscript is known to exist today.

5. *Lost Writings.* It is also true that some of the earlier "books" or writings referred to in the Bible have been lost, as is seen from the following quotations: "The Book of the Wars of Jehovah" (Num. 21:14); "The Book of Jasher" (Josh. 10:13 and II Sam. 1:18); "The Book of Iddo the Seer"

*Revised by Reverend Seaborn Kiker, Pastor of the Irwindell Methodist Church, Dallas, Texas.

(II Chron. 12:15) ; "The Book of Nathan" (I Chron. 29-29) ; and "The Book of Gad" (I Chron. 29-29).

6. *Manuscripts and Versions.* (1. The Septuagint—pronounced sep'-tu-a-gint.) Long before the time of Christ there was a great settlement of Jews in Alexandria, Egypt. Seventy Jewish scholars translated the sacred Scriptures into the Hellenistic Greek, the universal language of their day. This translation, known as the Septuagint, was used in the synagogues at the time of Christ. (2. Three Famous MSS.) According to the claim of scholars, copies out of the original languages are known as manuscripts, and translated into other languages are called versions. We have in existence today three very famous MSS.: (a) The Vatican, the earliest, has lain in the Vatican at Rome for something like 500 years. (b.) The Cinaitic, which was discovered by Dr. Tischendorf in St. Catherine's Monastery at Mt. Sinai. This is now in the British Museum, London. The story of the discovery and the recovery of this very ancient manuscript is as interesting as a novel. (c.) The Alexandrian. This manuscript was presented to Charles I by Cyril Lucar of Constantinople, 1628 A.D. It arrived in London seventeen years too late to be used in the making of the King James Version of the Bible. This manuscript is now kept in the British Museum. It is worthy of note that these three manuscripts are in the possession of the Roman Catholic church and the Protestant church. It is also worthy of note that none of these was available when the King James Version was written, but facsimile copies of these were in possession of those scholars who gave us the American Standard Version and other revised versions.

Among the many versions in which the Bible has been translated, one of the most famous is the Latin Vulgate, which was translated by the great Latin scholar, Jerome. This Latin Vulgate is practically the Bible of the Roman Catholic church today.

An important translation from the Latin Vulgate is the Douay Version, which is the standard ·Bible of the Catholic church. This version is to the Catholic church what the King James Version is to the Protestant church. Both of these important translations were completed about the same time,— the Douay, New Testament, 1582, and the Old Testament in 1609; the King James, in 1611. The Douay Version contains, in addition to the thirty-nine books found in the King James Version, some apocryphal books, such as I Maccabees and II Maccabees.

There are many other versions, such as the Syriac scriptures, the Egyptian, the Ethiopic, and Armenian. The later translations are those of Wycliffe, Tyndale, Coverdale, The Great Bible, The Geneva Bible, and our authorized Bible and the American Revised, etc. In addition to these splendid versions, we have the modern translation by individual scholars, such as the Moffatt and Goodspeed translations. Their main attempt is to translate the Bible into modern thought and language.

QUESTIONS

1. In what languages were the Old and the New Testament written?
2. What is the Septuagint?
3. Name three manuscripts, and tell where they are now.
4. Name three important versions.
5. What is the difference between manuscripts and versions?
6. What is the Douay Bible?
7. Name the scholars who have made recent translations of the Bible into modern English.

LITERARY CHARACTERISTICS OF THE BIBLE

By Dr. Umphrey Lee,
President of Southern Methodist University, Dallas

In our study of the Bible we must not neglect a consideration of its literary character. The English Bible has contributed more phrases to our common language, has stimulated the thinking of more of our writers, and has been the delight of more readers than any other book in our language. An appreciation of the different kinds of literature contained in this one volume, and the ability to read with pleasure its narratives, its poetry, and its letters should be a part of every educated man's acquirement. In this short essay, there will be pointed out only (1) the character of the language, (2) the nature of the poetry, and (3) the general literary types of the Bible.

1. *Language.* For our purpose the Bible is an English book; although the Old Testament was originally written almost altogether in Hebrew and the New Testament in Greek, and the two have been translated into almost every known language and dialect. Yet the Bible which most students will read is an English book. Because of this the language and style of the Bible are essentially the same throughout. Fortunately, our King James Version, the one most commonly used, was translated in a time, the so-called Eliza-

bethan Age, when the English language was yet simple and concrete, in every way fitted to translate the Hebrew and Greek of the Bible.

Ancient Hebrew was a language with few words for abstract ideas; most Hebrew words had "a physical significa- tion." A great French scholar illustrated this characteristic of Hebrew by calling attention to the way the Old Testament avoids the use of such comparatively simple abstractions as "discouragement," "despair," "pride." *Discouragement* and *despair* are expressed by the melting of the heart. *Pride* is portrayed by the holding high of the head, with the figure straight and stiff. *Patience* is a long breathing, *impatience* short breathing, *desire* is thirst or paleness. (Cf. Psalms 22:7, 14, 24.)

In the same way, the Greek language in which the New Testament was written was not the involved Greek of the classics, but a simple, popular tongue, spoken throughout the Mediterranean world in the centuries immediately preceding and succeeding the Christian era. If you read a few verses from John's Gospel, you will see the simplest form of this language: there are few dependent clauses, and the connec- tives are usually *and, but, for,* etc.

The student who would appreciate the peculiar fitness of Elizabethan English for the translation of the Bible should read the Dedicatory Letter to King James written by the translators in 1611, which is even yet printed in some copies of that version. Here they will find the rich, colorful phrases which we associate with Hebrew poetry and the concrete words which are characteristic both of the Bible and of Shake- speare.[1]

2. *Poetry.* In the vivid vocabulary of the Hebrew and Greek writers, the Bible contains a great deal of poetry. Therefore one who would read the Bible with pleasure must know how to distinguish prose from poetry and must learn to read the poetry with appreciation. English poetry is usully char- acterized by meter and rhyme, and even "free verse" is printed in a peculiar way. But the Hebrew poetry has neither rhyme nor meter (speaking generally), and in the older versions of the English Bible poetry and prose are printed alike. First, then, let us ask: What is the essential characteristic of Hebrew poetry?

If we turn to the Psalms, we can study the various ways in which the Hebrews varied their fundamental poetic principle.

---

[1]In this and other matters relating to the Bible as English literature, the student should consult J. H. Gardner, *The Bible as English Litera- ture.* New York, 1916.

The heavens declare the glory of god;
And the firmament sheweth his handy work. (Ps. 19:1.)

Here is the simplest form of Hebrew poetry, in which the second line of a couplet repeats the sense of the first line but in different words. Hebrew poetry consists in a "balance of thought contained in the words rather than in the balance of the number of syllables." This balance is called "parallelism."

Sometimes the second line adds to the thought of the first:

O clap your hands, all ye people;
Shout unto God with voice of triumph. (Ps. 47:1.)

Again, the second line will introduce a thought opposite to that set forth in the first:

For the Lord knoweth the way of the righteous:
But the way of the ungodly shall perish. (Ps. 1:6.)

Occasionally each line will develop something suggested by the preceding, thus building up the thought in a "stair-case" or "spiral" fashion, as in the following example:

I will lift up mine eyes unto the hills,
From whence cometh my help;
My help cometh from the Lord,
Which made heaven and earth. (Ps. 121:1.)

3. *Literary Types.* To understand and read with pleasure the Bible one should recognize the *different types of literature* which are found in it. There are *narratives* such as the stories of Joseph (Genesis 37, 39-46), and of David (I and II Samuel). There are *lyrics* such as the Psalms and other short poems scattered through the historical and prophetic books. The Book of Job is a *dramatic poem,* in which different characters are introduced, who express their views in long poetic speeches. Much of the Old Testament is taken up by books which we call *prophetic.* These—Amos, Hosea, Micah, Isaiah, Jeremiah, etc.—are deliverances by the "prophets" on religious, moral, and political conditions of their times, with predictions of the course of events under certain moral conditions. In the New Testament, we have the *Gospels,* accounts of the Life and Teachings of Jesus, and the *Letters* (usually called Epistles) mainly written by Paul. These latter are real letters with salutations and formal endings such as were common in that day.

The student who seeks an appreciation of the literary character of the Bible should study one or two of the Psalms for examples of parallelism. He should glance through some modern edition of the Bible which prints the poetical section in the form of poetry, in order that he may see how much of the Bible is poetical. To distinguish the different types of literature in the Bible, the student should read some narratives; as the story of Joseph, the Prophecy of Amos, at least a part of the Book of Job, the Gospel according to Mark, and the Epistle of Philemon.

QUESTIONS

1. Give several important characteristics of Hebrew poetry. What is the most common characteristic?
2. Compare English and Hebrew poetry.
3. Give three examples of Hebrew poetry. (See "Psalms," pages 35-36.)
4. Name and give an example of five literary types in the Bible.

BIBLE HISTORY, A HISTORY OF REDEMPTION

By T. M. DALTON,

Teacher of Bible Credit Classes in the First Methodist Church, Dallas, Texas; Author of A Comprehensive Bible Study Course

It is not the purpose of the writers of the Bible to write the history of the world. It is not their purpose to write even the history of mankind. Their object is to write the history of redemption. Starting from the broad fact of man's separation from God, they trace that element of human history which results in the perfect reunion of God and man. The keynote was struck in the promise that the seed of the woman should prevail over the seed of the serpent (Gen. 3:15), that the effects of man's voluntary separation from God might be removed. It is the fulfillment of this promise which is traced by the sacred writers. They steadily pursue that one line of history which runs directly toward this fulfillment, often turning aside to pursue to a greater or less distance, diverging lines, but always returning to the grand highway on which this promise travels. Accordingly, the first eleven chapters of Genesis, though turning aside from time to time from this main purpose, to set down the history of such important collateral matters as Cain and Abel, the flood, the origin of nations, and the Tower of Babel, trace the line of promise from Adam, through Seth, to Noah (Gen. 5), and from Noah, through Shem to Abraham (Gen. 11:10 to 32).

With Abraham there opens a new chapter in the history of man's redemption from sin. The promise of redemption through the seed of the woman, given at the time of man's fall, was renewed and confined to Abraham and his descendants in God's promise to Abraham, "And in thy seed shall all the nations of the earth be blessed" (Gen. 22:18). So, from the time of God's covenant with Abraham to its ultimate fulfillment in Christ (Gal. 3:16), the history of redemption is inseparably connected with the history of Abraham and his descendants, the Hebrew people. In fact, Bible history, being given by inspiration of God, has for its main object the unfolding of God's progressive revelation of Himself, as man's Savior and Redeemer, made to the seed of Abraham, and to record the way in which that revelation was received, and the effects which it produced. It was God's pleasure to reveal himself in connection with the history of a nation through announcements and institutions and practical dealings, bearing in the first instance on them. Bible history, therefore, must be studied in connection with God's main purpose, the revelation of Himself as man's Savior and Redeemer, and the supernatural interpositions by which from time to time that purpose was carried out.

In accord with the Divine purpose of tracing the progressive unfolding of the plan of redemption, the Pentateuch forms a consecutive whole. After removing the story of the creation and the history of the primitive world, it passed on to deal more especially with the history of the Hebrew people. It gives at some length the personal history of the three great fathers of the family, Abraham, Isaac, and Jacob. It then describes how the family grew into a nation in Egypt, telling us of its oppression and deliverance, of its forty years' wandering in the wilderness, of the giving of the law with all its enactments (both civil and religious), of the construction of the tabernacle, of the numbering of the people, of the rights and duties of the priesthood, as well as of many important events which befell them before their entrance into the land of Canaan, and finally concludes with Moses's last discourses and death. Thus, the Pentateuch traces the history of the progressive fulfillment of the Covenant with Abraham from the call of Abraham (Gen. 12:1 to 3), to the preparation of the nation on the plains of Moab for entrance into the Promised Land.

The Book of Joshua, taking up the history where the Pentateuch leaves off, records the history of fulfillment of the divine promise to Abraham, "I will give unto thee, and to thy seed after thee, the land wherein thou art a stranger, all the land of Canaan, for an everlasting possession" (Gen. 17:8). Judges, Ruth, I Samuel, II Samuel, and I Chronicles trace through many vicissitudes the fulfillment of God's promise to Abraham, "I will make of thee a great nation" (Gen. 12:2), from the death of Joshua to the peak of Israel's national greatness under David.

All the history of the Hebrew people from Abraham to David constitutes the first epoch of the fulfillment of God's promise to Abraham, "In thy seed shall all the nations of the

earth be blessed" (Gen. 22:18). This promise as renewed to
David (II Samuel 7:16) indicated that the blessing to the
nations should come through a king of his line. The promise,
as made to Abraham, and renewed to David, constitutes the
mission and the hope of Israel.

I Kings, II Kings, and II Chronicles trace the unfolding of
the promise to David, "And thine house and thy kingdom shall
be established forever before thee: thy throne shall be established forever" (II Samuel 7:16), from David until the carry-
ing away into Babylon. God's continued faithfulness to this
promise, in spite of the sins and unfaithfulness of many of
those whom it most concerned, is evidenced by the fact that
from Jeroboam to the Assyrian captivity of the Ten Tribes,
Israel was ruled by nine dynasties, while from Rehoboam to
the Babylonian captivity Judah was ruled only by the house
of David. The period covered by these books constitutes the
second epoch of the fulfillment of the divine promise to Abraham.

Ezra, Nehemiah, Esther, and the historical portions of Daniel and other prophets deal with the third and final epoch of
the progressive fulfillment of God's covenant with Abraham,
which had its beginning with the Babylonian captivity, and its
ending with the birth of Christ. God's providential dealings
with Israel during this period accomplished two important
results. It cured the people of idolatry forever; thus on the
fragments of the political kingdom of Israel establishing for
the first time the spiritual kingdom of God. The other great
result was the Dispersion. Only a small remnant of the people
came back to Palestine. The rest remained in Babylon or were
scattered abroad among the nations of the earth. These Jews
in their dispersion became a Church in the world, the original
type of the Church of Christ and the soil out of which it
sprang. Thus out of the chastening of this final period of the
fulfillment of the promise to Abraham sprang the spiritual
kingdom as distinguished from the political kingdom, and the
world-wide Church as distinguished from the merely national
Church, completing the preparation for the Coming of Christ,
in whom alone was and is the ultimate fulfillment of God's
promise to Abraham, "In thy seed shall all the nations of the
earth be blessed" (Galatians 3:8 to 16).

QUESTIONS

1. What is the chief purpose underlying Biblical history?
2. Trace the progressive unfolding of the plan of redemption as related
   to Abraham, Joshua, David, and Ezra.
3. How many epochs are there in the progressive fulfillment of God's
   covenant with Abraham?
4. Name two important results of the Babylonian captivity.

THE OLD TESTAMENT CANON
(THE HEBREW BIBLE)

The Jewish Canon (Bible) at the time of Christ contained the books of our Old Testament but grouped as twenty-four books instead of thirty-nine, under three main divisions as follows (Dummelow, *Bible Commentary*, page xii) :

1. Books of Law (5)—Genesis, Exodus, Leviticus, Numbers, Deuteronomy.

2. Prophets (8)—Arranged under two groups.
   a. Earlier—Joshua, Judges, Samuel, Kings.
   b. Later—Isaiah, Jeremiah, Ezekiel, and the twelve prophets.

3. Writings (11)—arranged under three groups.
   a. Psalms, Proverbs, and Job.
   b. Song of Solomon, Ruth, Lamentations, Ecclesiastes, Esther.
   c. Daniel, Ezra and Nehemiah, and Chronicles.

It is believed by Christians that Jesus gave His approval to these groupings, when after His resurrection He said to His disciples: "These are the words which I spake unto you, while I was yet with you, that all things must be fulfilled, which were written in the law of Moses, and in the prophets and in the psalms, concerning me." Luke 24:44.

QUESTIONS

1. How many main divisions were there in the Old Testament Canon? Name these.

2. How many different books in the Old Testament Canon?

In what light soever we regard the Bible, whether with reference to revelation, to history, to morality, it is an invaluable and an inexhaustible mine of knowledge and virtue.

JOHN QUINCY ADAMS.

CLASSIFICATION OF THE BOOKS OF THE BIBLE

(COMMON ARRANGEMENT)

OLD TESTAMENT (39 books)

1. Law (5) : Genesis, Exodus, Leviticus, Numbers, Deuteronomy. (These are called the Pentateuch.)

2. History (12) : Joshua, Judges, Ruth, I Samuel, II Samuel, I Kings, II Kings, I Chronicles, II Chronicles, Ezra, Nehemiah, Esther.

3. Poetry (5) : Job, Psalms, Proverbs, Ecclesiastes, Song of Solomon.

4. Major Prophets (5) : Isaiah, Jeremiah, Lamentations, Ezekiel, Daniel.

5. Minor Prophets (12) : Hosea, Joel, Amos, Obadiah, Jonah, Micah, Nahum, Habakkuk, Zephaniah, Haggai, Zechariah, Malachi.

NEW TESTAMENT (27 books)

1. Biography (4 Gospels) : Matthew, Mark, Luke, John.

2. History: Acts.

3. Pauline Letters (14) : Romans, I Corinthians, II Corinthians, Galatians, Ephesians, Philippians, Colossians, I Thessalonians, II Thessalonians, I Timothy, II Timothy, Titus, Philemon, Hebrews (generally ascribed to Paul).

4. General Letters (7) : James, I Peter, II Peter, I John, II John, III John, Jude.

5. Prophecy: Revelation.

QUESTIONS

1. How many books in the Old Testament? In the New Testament?

2. Classify the books of the Old Testament; name and give the number of books in each group.

3. Classify the books of the New Testament; name and give the number of books in each group.

REQUIRED MEMORY WORK
(For Review Purposes)

Every pupil should be able to reproduce accurately from memory the following:

1. The names and classifications of the books of the Bible:
   a. Old Testament (39 books)
      (1) Law (5): Genesis, Exodus, Leviticus, Numbers, Deuteronomy
      (2) History (12): Joshua, Judges, Ruth, I Samuel, II Samuel, I Kings, II Kings, I Chronicles, II Chronicles, Ezra, Nehemiah, Esther
      (3) Poetry (5): Job, Psalms, Proverbs, Ecclesiastes, Song of Solomon
      (4) Major Prophets (5): Isaiah, Jeremiah, Lamentations, Ezekiel, Daniel
      (5) Minor Prophets, (12): Hosea, Joel, Amos, Obadiah, Jonah, Micah, Nahum, Habakkuk, Zephaniah, Haggai, Zechariah, Malachi
   b. New Testament (27 books)
      (1) Biography (4 Gospels): Matthew, Mark, Luke, John
      (2) History: Acts
      (3) Pauline Letters (14): Romans, I Corinthians, II Corinthians, Galatians, Ephesians, Philippians, Colossians, I Thessalonians, II Thessalonians, I Timothy, II Timothy, Titus, Philemon, Hebrews (generally ascribed to Paul)
      (4) General Letters (7): James, I Peter, II Peter, I John, II John, III John, Jude
      (5) Prophecy: Revelation

2. The names of the Tribes of Israel (twelve sons of Jacob): Reuben, Simeon, Levi, Judah, Issachar, Zebulon, Dan, Naphtali, Gad, Asher, Joseph, Benjamin

3. Genesis 1:1
   "In the beginning God created the heaven and the earth."
   (Spoken by Moses, the author, concerning the creation)

4. Genesis 3:12
   "The woman whom thou gavest to be with me, she gave me of the tree, and I did eat."

5. Genesis 3:19
   "In the sweat of thy face thou shalt eat bread."

6. Genesis 3:19
   "Dust thou art, and unto dust thou shalt return."

7. Genesis 4:9
   "Am I my brother's keeper?" ·

8. Genesis 4:10
   "The voice of thy brother's blood crieth unto me from the ground."

9. Numbers 6:24-26. The Aaronic Benediction:
   "The Lord bless thee and keep thee:
   The Lord make his face shine upon thee, and be gracious unto thee:
   The Lord lift up his countenance upon thee, and give thee peace."
   (Through Moses God gave this benediction to Aaron to use in blessing the Children of Israel.)

10. Exodus 20:1-21. The Ten Commandments:
    a. Thou shalt have no other Gods before Me.
    b. Thou shalt not make unto thee any graven image, or any likeness of any thing . . .
       Thou shalt not bow down thyself to them, nor serve them; . . .
    c. Thou shalt not take the name of the Lord thy God in vain: for the Lord will not hold him guiltless that taketh his name in vain.
    d. Remember the sabbath day, to keep it holy. Six days shalt thou labor, and do all thy work. But the seventh day is the sabbath of the Lord thy God: in it thou shalt not do any work, . . .
    e. Honor thy father and thy mother: that thy days may be long upon the land which the Lord thy God giveth thee.
    f. Thou shalt not kill.
    g. Thou shalt not commit adultery.
    h. Thou shalt not steal.
    i. Thou shalt not bear false witness against thy neighbor.
    j. Thou shalt not covet . . . any thing that is thy neighbor's.
       (Spoken by God to Moses.) Note: The Ten Commandments were given on tablets of stone by God to Moses and were written by God's own finger. Exodus 24:12; 31-18; 34:1.

11. I Samuel 3:10
    "Speak, for thy servant heareth."
    (The child, Samuel, in answer to the Lord's call to him.)

12. Psalm 1

> Blessed is the man that walketh not in the counsel of the ungodly, nor standeth in the way of sinners, nor sitteth in the seat of the scornful.
>
> But his delight is in the law of the Lord: and in his law doth he meditate day and night.
>
> And he shall be like a tree planted by the rivers of water, that bringeth forth his fruit in his season; his leaf also shall not wither; and whatsoever he doeth shall prosper.
>
> The ungodly are not so: but are like the chaff which the wind driveth away.
>
> Therefore the ungodly shall not stand in the judgment, nor sinners in the congregation of the righteous.
>
> For the Lord knoweth the way of the righteous: but the way of the ungodly shall perish.
> (Spoken by the Psalmist David)

13. Psalm 19:14

> Let the words of my mouth, and the meditation of my heart, be acceptable in thy sight, O Lord, my strength, and my redeemer. (Spoken by the Psalmist David)

14. Psalm 23

> The Lord is my shepherd; I shall not want.
>
> He maketh me to lie down in green pastures: he leadeth me beside the still waters.
>
> He restoreth my soul: he leadeth me in the paths of righteousness for his name's sake.
>
> Yea, though I walk through the valley of the shadow of death, I will fear no evil: for thou art with me; thy rod and thy staff they comfort me.
>
> Thou preparest a table before me in the presence of mine enemies: thou anointest my head with oil; my cup runneth over.
>
> Surely goodness and mercy shall follow me all the days of my life: and I will dwell in the house of the Lord forever. (Spoken by the Psalmist David)

15. Psalm 91:1-2, 11

> He that dwelleth in the secret place of the most High shall abide under the shadow of the Almighty.
>
> I will say of the Lord, He is my refuge and my fortress: my God; in him will I trust.
>
> For he shall give his angels charge over thee, to keep thee in all thy ways. (Psalmist unknown)

16. Psalm 100

   Make a joyful noise unto the Lord, all ye lands.

   Serve the Lord with gladness: come before his presence with singing.

   Know ye that the Lord he is God: it is he that hath made us and not we ourselves: we are his people and the sheep of his pasture.

   Enter into his gates with thanksgiving, and into his courts with praise: be thankful unto him, and bless his name.

   For the Lord is good; his mercy is everlasting; and his truth endureth to all generations.

   (Psalmist unknown)

17. Proverbs 3:5-6

   Trust in the Lord with all thine heart; and lean not unto thine own understanding.

   In all thy ways acknowledge him, and he shall direct thy paths.

   (Spoken by Solomon)

18. Ecclesiastes 12:1

   Remember now thy Creator in the days of thy youth, while the evil days come not, nor the years draw nigh, when thou shalt say, I have no pleasure in them.

   (Spoken by Solomon, the author of Ecclesiastes.)

19. Ecclesiastes 12:13

   . . . Fear God, and keep his commandments: for this is the whole duty of man.

   (Spoken by Solomon, the author of Ecclesiastes.)

20. Micah 6:8

   He hath shewed thee, O man, what is good; and what doth the Lord require of thee, but to do justly, and to love mercy, and to walk humbly with thy God?

   (The prophet, Micah, speaking to Judah and Israel.)

21. Matthew 22:37-40

   Jesus said unto him, Thou shalt love the Lord thy God with all thy heart, and with all thy soul, and with all thy mind.

   This is the first and great commandment.

   And the second is like unto it, Thou shalt love thy neighbor as thyself.

   On these two commandments hang all the law and the prophets.

   (Jesus' reply to a lawyer who attempted to test him.)

22. II Timothy 2:15
   Study to shew thyself approved unto God, a workman
   that needeth not to be ashamed, rightly dividing the
   word of truth.
   (The Apostle Paul's advice to the young minister, Timothy.)

23. II Timothy 3:16
   All scripture is given by inspiration of God, and is
   profitable for doctrine, for reproof, for correction, for
   instruction in righteousness:
   (The Apostle Paul to the young minister, Timothy.)

24. II Peter 1:21
   For the prophecy came not in old time by the will of man:
   but holy men of God spake as they were moved by
   the Holy Ghost.
   (Peter's explanation of the origin of the Bible.)

SPECIMEN EXAMINATION QUESTIONS

FINAL EXAMINATION IN OLD TESTAMENT
MAY 8, 1943

I—Value 10 (½ each)

Name below the common classifications, or divisions, of the
books of the Old Testament, and give three examples of each
division.

Divisions of Old Testament	*Examples of each division*
1.	
2.	
3.	
4.	
5.	

II—Value 10 (½ each)

The outline of the text (Old Testament Bible Study Course)
comprises six periods or divisions, the last being the Fulfillment of Old Testament Prophecies. (1) Write these six divisions in proper sequence, putting the earliest first, and so on.
(2) Write the following names and events after the proper
period: Lot, Esau, Tower of Babel, The Plagues, Rachel,
Noah, Cyrus, Saul, John the Baptist, Rehoboam, Jonathan,
Daniel, Exodus, Conquest of Canaan.

1. _____   _____
2. _____   _____
3. _____   _____
4. _____   _____
5. _____   _____
6. _____   _____

III—Value 10 (½ each)

Write in the blanks below the author or speaker of any 20 of the following quotations:

1. _____ "Let my people go."

2. _____ "Thou art the man."

3. _____ "Am I my brother's keeper?"

4. _____ "Behold the dreamer cometh."

5. _____ "To obey is better than sacrifice."

6. _____ "Hitherto hath the Lord helped us."

7. _____ "Canst thou by searching find out God?"

8. _____ "Be strong and quit yourselves like men."

9. _____ "Though He slay me, yet will I trust Him."

10. _____ "My spirit shall not always strive with man."

11. _____ "God did send me before you to preserve life."

12. _____ "I have built a house for the name of the Lord."

13. _____ "Thy people shall be my people, and thy God my God."

14. _____ "Wist ye not that I must be about my Father's business?"

15. _____ "So built we the wall; for the people had a mind to work."

16. _____ "Whatsoever thy hand findeth to do, do it with thy might."

17. _____ "The Lord shall fight for you, and ye shall hold your peace."

18. _____ "Not by might nor by power, but by my spirit, saith the Lord of hosts."

19. _____ "Let us go up at once and possess it; for we are well able to overcome it."

20. _____ "Cast thy bread upon the waters; for thou shalt find it after many days."

21. _____ "Thou shalt call His name Jesus, for He shall save His people from their sins."

22. _____ "The Lord watch between me and thee when we are absent one from the other."

IV—Value 10 (½ each)

Supply the missing word or words in any 20 of the following:

1. _____ befriended the spies.

2. _____ was the father of the Hebrew nation.

3. _____ won with an army of three hundred.

4. _____ was the immediate successor of Moses.

5. _____ stole his brother's blessing.

6. _____ interpreted Nebuchadnezzar's dream.

7. _____ was famed for his great physical strength.

8. _____ was the sister of Moses.

9. _____ rebuilt the walls of Jerusalem.

10. _____ was called on to sacrifice his own son.

11. _____ was the last and greatest of the Judges.

12. _____ was the faithful friend of David.

13. A soft answer_____

14. They that sow in tears_____

15. In the sweat of thy face_____

16. Canst thou by searching_____

17. Daniel purposed in his heart that_____

18. Can two walk together except_____

19. A good name is rather to be chosen_____

20. Thy word have I hid in my heart that_____

21. Keep thy heart with all diligence, for_____

22. The fear of the Lord is_____

V—Value 10 (½ each)

In any 10 of the blanks below, write the *number* of the book or individual given in the second column which best matches the thought expressed in the first column. The first blank is filled out correctly to show what is meant.

(5) Instructions to the priests
_____ Problem of human suffering
_____ Prayer book and hymnal of the Hebrews
_____ Maxims on right living
_____ Vanity of human life
_____ Exilic prophet
_____ Pre-exilic prophet
_____ Post-exilic prophet
_____ Love story of a gentile maiden
_____ Book of beginnings, or origins
_____ Forerunner of Christ
_____ Account of deliverance of the Hebrews from Egypt
_____ Beautiful poem of loyalty and faithfulness

1. Exodus
2. Ecclesiastes
3. Psalms
4. Genesis
5. Leviticus
6. Proverbs
7. Haggai
8. Jeremiah
9. Daniel
10. Job
11. Ruth
12. Esther
13. Amos
14. Joshua
15. Song of Solomon
16. John the Baptist

VI—Value 10 (½ each)

Write a check mark (√) in the proper blank for any 20 of the following to show whether statement is true or false. An example is given to show what is meant.

True False

√ _____ _____ Moses wrote the Pentateuch.

1. _____ _____ Hebrew poetry contains neither rhythm nor meter.
2. _____ _____ The Amalekites were a peace-loving people.
3. _____ _____ The Kingdom of Judah outlived the Kingdom of Israel.
4. _____ _____ The Feast of the Passover commemorates the Exodus.
5. _____ _____ Jerusalem is on the Jordan River.
6. _____ _____ The Ark of the Covenant was kept in the Most Holy Place.
7. _____ _____ Jericho successfully resisted the siege of the Hebrews led by Joshua.
8. _____ _____ Lot and Isaac were brothers.
9. _____ _____ Manna ceased after the Israelites entered Canaan.
10. _____ _____ Cities of refuge were places of protection.

11. ____ ____ The Northern Kingdom was conquered by Assyria.

12. ____ ____ The "lost tribes of Israel" were ten in number.

13. ____ ____ The plagues occurred during the wilderness experiences of the Hebrews.

14. ____ ____ The Septuagint is a translation of the Hebrew scriptures into Latin.

15. ____ ____ The burial place of Moses is frequently visited by tourists.

16. ____ ____ At the birth of Jesus use of the Greek language was widespread.

17. ____ ____ The Southern Kingdom comprised the tribes of Judah and Benjamin.

18. ____ ____ Monotheism is a belief in one god.

19. ____ ____ The Tower of Babel was in Egypt.

20. ____ ____ Canaan was divided equally among the twelve tribes.

21. ____ ____ Moses led the Hebrews through the land of the Phillistines.

22. ____ ____ Samson frequently fought the Phillistines.

VII—Value 10 (½ each)

(a) Write in the blanks the *number* of the *correct term* in any 10 of the following. An example is given to show what is meant.

(4) Abraham's earliest home: (1) Haran, (2) Egypt, (3) Hebron, (4) Ur.

1. ____ The beloved wife of Jacob: (1) Sarah, (2) Rachel, (3) Hannah, (4) Deborah.

2. ____ Moses viewed Canaan from: (1) Mt. Sinai, (2) Mt. Nebo, (3) Mt. Hermon.

3. ____ Noah's Ark landed on: (1) Mt. Sinai, (2) Mt. Hor, (3) Mt. Hermon, (4) Mt. Ararat.

4. ____ First King of Israel: (1) Jethro, (2) David, (3) Saul.

5. ____ The Hebrews were descendants of: (1) Ham, (2) Shem, (3) Japheth, (4) Seth.

6. _____ Priests were taken from tribe of: (1) Judah, (2) Benjamin, (3) Levi, (4) Ephraim.

7. _____ First in point of time: (1) Solomon, (2) Joseph, (3) Isaac, (4) Moses.

8. _____ Last in point of time: (1) Boaz, (2) Ezra, (3) Solomon, (4) Isaac.

9. _____ Queen who visited Solomon: (1) Esther, (2) Sheba, (3) Vashti.

10. _____ The kingdom was divided during the reign of: (1) Saul, (2) David, (3) Rehoboam, (4) Solomon.

11. _____ Lived after the Patriarchal Period: (1) Abraham, (2) Isaac, (3) Jacob, (4) Joseph, (5) Saul.

12. _____ Ruth became the wife of: (1) Elimelech, (2) Boaz, (3) Samson, (4) Gideon.

(b) Write in the blanks the *number* of the *incorrect term* in any 10 of the following.

1. _____ Assisted the Jews in return from exile: (1) Ezra, (2) Cyrus, (3) Zerubbabel, (4) Malachi.

2. _____ Tribes in the Northern Kingdom: (1) Judah, (2) Dan, (3) Gad, (4) Reuben.

3. _____ Women of the Old Testament: (1) Naomi, (2) Esther, (3) Elizabeth, (4) Deborah.

4. _____ Persons whose names were changed: (1) Jacob, (2) Isaac, (3) Abram, (4) Sarai.

5. _____ Important judges of Israel: (1) Gideon, (2) Deborah, (3) Joshua, (4) Samuel.

6. _____ Went to Heaven without dying: (1) Enoch, (2) Elijah, (3) Elisha.

7. _____ Major prophets: (1) Isaiah, (2) Hosea, (3) Daniel, (4) Jeremiah.

8. _____ Minor prophets: (1) Ezekiel, (2) Amos, (3) Zechariah, (4) Nahum.

9. _____ Moses was great as: (1) leader, (2) emancipator, (3) law-giver, (4) orator.

10. _____ Historical books of the Bible: (1) Judges, (2) Joel, (3) Joshua, (4) Ruth.

11. _____ Poetical books of the Bible: (1) Job, (2) Psalms, (3) Exodus, (4) Proverbs, (5) Ecclesiastes.

VIII—Value 10

Quote or give substance of the Ten Commandments. **List** in order. (Value 1 each)

1. _____
2. _____
3. _____
4. _____
5. _____
6. _____
7. _____
8. _____
9. _____
10. _____

IX—Value 10 (2 each)

Quote accurately the following:

Gen. 1:1
Psalm 23:1-4 or Psalm 1:5-6
Micah 6:8
Ecc. 12:13
II Tim. 2:15 or II Peter 1:21

X—Value 10 (1 each)

On the map given locate any 10 of the following by writing in the proper place on the map the *number* (figure) placed in *front* of each term: (1) Mediterranean Sea, (2) Dead Sea, (3) Sea of Galilee, (4) Jordan River, (5) Mt. Carmel, (6) Beer-Sheba, (7) Hebron, (8) Bethlehem, (9) Jericho, (10) Tyre, (11) the three chief divisions of Palestine in New Testament times. For number 11 draw boundary lines and write names of divisions.

The Bible ought to be read, were it only for the sake of the grand English in which it is written.
ALFRED TENNYSON.

The statutes of the Lord are right, rejoicing the heart: the commandment of the Lord is pure, enlightening the eyes. (Psalms 19:8.)

GLOSSARY

Abraham (ā′brȧ-hăm) (*father of a multitude*). A descendant of Noah, appointed by God to be the founder of the Hebrew race.

Abram (ā′brăm) (*lofty father*). The original name of Abraham.

Adam (ăd′ăm) (*man*). The name which God gave to man and woman. (Gen. 5:2).

Adullam (ȧ-dŭl′lŭm). A cave about ten miles northwest of Hebron. David killed Goliath near this cave and later took refuge there when he fled from the wrath of Saul.

altar (ôl′tẽr). A raised place, structure or elevation of earth or stone for offering of sacrifices or burning of incense; a place of worship.

Apocrypha (ȧ-pŏk′rĭ-fȧ) (*hidden secret*). Fourteen books which the Jews and the early Christian fathers considered to be without divine authority. They were included in the Septuagint. All except two are in the Latin Vulgate, the Roman Catholic Bible.

Ararat (âr′ȧ-răt). The resting place of the ark after the flood, commonly believed to be a mountain in Armenia.

Babel, The Tower of (bā′bĕl) (*bab-il, the gate of God; confusion*). A tower built in the land of Shinar by the descendants of Noah, who expected by means of it to ascend into heaven in case of another flood.

Babylon (băb′ĭ lŏn). One of the oldest cities in Mesopotamia (in Genesis called Shinar), founded by Nimrod, the hunter and the great-grandson of Noah.

Bethel (bĕth′-ĕl) (*house of God*). A sacred place where Jacob had the vision of the ladder. He called it *house of God* because he heard God's voice there.

Bethlehem (bĕth′lĕ-hĕm) (*house of bread*). A city about five miles south of Jerusalem. It was the birthplace of Naomi, Boaz, David, and Jesus. It was the burial place of Rachel, Jacob's favorite wife.

Bible (bī′b'l) (*book, papyrus*). The name given to the books of the Old and New Testaments, the sacred writings accepted by Christians as inspired by God and of divine authority. Other names applied to the Bible are the Scriptures, the Word, the Covenants, and the Law.

canon (kăn′ŭn) (*a measuring rod, a rule*). The books of the Bible recognized by the Christian Church as the inspired rule of faith and practice; also the catalogue or list of these books.

Chaldea (kăl-dē′a). The southern portion of Babylonia bordering on the Persian Gulf.

cherubim (chĕr′ŭ-bĭm). Winged symbolical figures frequently mentioned in the Scriptures. When Adam and Eve were expelled from the Garden of Eden, cherubim guarded the east gate with a flaming sword. Two were placed on the Mercy Seat of the Ark of the Covenant.

covenant (kŭv′e-nănt) (*agreement*). A compact or agreement between two parties. As between God and man, it is God's promise of blessing to be fulfilled on the performance of a condition. The Old Covenant is the Old Testament; the New Covenant is the New Testament.

Damascus (dà-màs′kŭs). An ancient city of Syria about fifty miles east of the Mediterranean coast and 140 miles northeast of Jerusalem. According to Josephus, it was founded by Uz, a grandson of Shem. It is first mentioned in Hebrew history in connection with Abraham in Genesis 15:2.

Decalogue (dĕk′à-lŏg) (*ten words*). The Ten Commandments which God gave Moses on Mount Sinai. (Exodus 20:1-17.)

Deuteronomy (dū′tĕr-ŏn-o-mĭ) (*second law*). The fifth book of Pentateuch, consisting largely of discourses delivered by Moses in the last year of his life. It is a restatement of the Mosaic Law.

Ebal, Mount (ē´bal). Ebal and Gerizim are mountains near the geographical center of Canaan. Joshua gathered the children of Israel in the hollow between the two mountains and in great solemnity read to them the Law of Moses. Half stood on the slope of Mount Ebal and half on Mount Gerizim. After the Captivity, Gerizim became the site of the Samaritan temple.

Edom (ē´dom) (*red*). The name given to Esau when he sold his birthright to Jacob for a bowl of lentil pottage. The red color of the food gave rise to the name. The Edomites were the descendants of Esau, or Edom.

epilogue (ĕp´ĭ-lŏg). A concluding section of a poem, speech, or discourse.

Euphrates (ū-frā´tēz). The most important river of western Asia. It rises in the Armenian mountains and flows into the Persian Gulf. It is one of the four rivers of the Garden of Eden.

Eve (*the mother of all living.*) The name Adam gave his wife. (Genesis 3:20.)

exile (ĕk´sīl). A person who is expelled, banished, or carried captive from his own country.

Exodus (ĕk´sō-dŭs *or* ĕks´ō-dŭs) (*going out*). The departure of the Israelites from Egypt and their journey to the Promised Land. The book of Exodus gives accounts of Israel's struggles for freedom from Egyptian bondage, the receiving of the Law on Mount Sinai, and the setting up of the Tabernacle.

firmament (fûr´ma-mĕnt). The arch or dome of the sky; the heavens. The Hebrews, like other primitive people, thought of the sky as a solid arched dome.

Genesis (jĕn´ē-sĭs) (*beginnings*). The first book of the Pentateuch which records the origin of the universe, the human race, sin, redemption, family life, nations, languages, and the Hebrew race.

gentile (jĕn´tīl) (*foreigner or heathen*). A term used by the Hebrews to refer to any people other than themselves.

Gerizim (gĕr′ĭ-zĭm). See *Ebal*.

Gilboa (gĭl-bō′à) (*bubbling spring*). A mountainous district in Manasseh west of the Jordan overlooking the city of Jezreel. Saul and Jonathan fell at Gilboa when the Israelites were defeated by the Philistines.

Gilgal (gĭl′găl). A hill west of the Jordan River and east of Jericho, where the Israelites spent their first night after crossing the Jordan. The first Passover Feast in the Land of Canaan was observed at Gilgal, and the first Hebrew king was crowned there.

Goshen (gō′shĕn). The name of the land in northern Egypt occupied by the Israelites. It was a fertile pasture land which extended probably from the Nile River to the Red Sea.

Haran (hā′răn). A place in north Mesopotamia to which Abraham and his family migrated from Ur of the Chaldees. Abraham's brother, Nahor, established himself at Haran. It was the home of Rebekah, Isaac's wife and of Laban, Jacob's father-in-law.

Hebrew (hē′brōō) (*crosser over*). A term applied to Abraham when he came to Canaan. He had *crossed over* the Euphrates River. *Hebrew* was the name by which the Israelites were known to foreigners.

Hebron (hē′bron). One of the oldest cities of Canaan about twenty miles south of Jerusalem. When Abraham first entered the Promised Land, he built an altar at Hebron. Caleb claimed Hebron when the land was divided among the Twelve Tribes. See *Macpelah*.

Ishmael (ĭsh′mȧ-ĕl). The first-born son of Abraham by Hagar, an Egyptian concubine. He is the progenitor of the Ishmaelites, known today as Bedouin Arabs.

Israel (ĭs′rȧ-ĕl) (*one who strives with God*). The name given to Jacob after his wrestling with the angel at Peniel. This was the name given to the family of Jacob, known as the Twelve Tribes of Israel. It was also the name of the Northern Kingdom made up of ten tribes.

Jericho (Jĕr'ĭ-kō). The first city taken by Joshua after crossing the Jordan. It was about six miles north-west of the Dead Sea and about five miles west of the Jordan.

Jerusalem (jê-rōō'sà-lĕm). The most sacred city of biblical history. It is about twenty miles west of the northern end of the Dead Sea. When the Israelites entered Canaan under the leadership of Joshua, it was held by the Jebusites. King David conquered the city and made it his capital in the eighth year of his reign. It was built upon four hills, the most famous of which is Mount Moriah. (See *Mount Moriah*.)

Joshua, The Book of (jŏsh'u-à). An account of the conquest and division of Canaan under the leadership of Joshua.

Judges, The Book of. The history of Israel from the death of Joshua to the accession of Saul, during which time fifteen so-called judges were the spiritual and political leaders.

Kadesh-barnea (kā'dĕsh-bär'ne a). A place on the southern frontier of Canaan. The second summer after the Israelites left Egypt, they encamped at Ka-desh-barnea. It was here that the rock was smitten for water; the twelve spies were sent from this place into Canaan; and Miriam was buried here.

Kings, The Books of I and II. A history of Israel from the reign of Solomon to the destruction of Jerusalem and the Babylonian captivity. Elijah and Elisha are the most heroic figures.

laver (lā'vẽr). A brass vessel containing water in which the priests were to bathe their hands and feet before sacrifices. In the Tabernacle there was one laver; in the Temple there were ten.

Lebanon (lĕb'à-nŭn). A double mountain range north of Palestine extending through Syria and lying paral-lel to the Mediterranean Sea.

Leviticus (lê-vĭt'ĭ-cŭs). The third book of the Penta-teuch, so named because it consists of instructions to the Levites and priests for the services in the place of worship.

Lost Tribes. A title given to the ten tribes of Israel (Northern Kingdom) who were never restored to their land after the Assyrian captivity.

Machpelah (măk-pē′lah). A plot of ground in Hebron where Abraham, Sarah, Isaac, Rebekah, Jacob, Leah, and perhaps Joseph are buried. It is thought to be the oldest cemetery in the world.

manna (măn′ă) (*What is this?*). Food which God miraculously gave to the Israelites during their forty years in the wilderness. It was so called because when the people first saw it upon the ground, they exclaimed, "What is this?" In form it resembled small white seed. It was ground and made into bread which tasted like wafers made with fresh oil and honey. (Ex. 16:14-36; Num. 11:8.)

Mesopotamia (mĕs′o-po-tā′mi-ă) (*between the rivers*). The land between the Tigris and Euphrates rivers.

Midian (mĭd′i-ăn). A land which included the Sinaitic Peninsula and extended east to the Euphrates River. It was the land to which Moses fled when he killed the Egyptian. The Midianites were the descendants of Abraham and Keturah. Jethro, Moses' father-in-law was a Midianite.

miracle (mĭr′ă-k′l). An event which happens through Divine intervention, the explanation of which is beyond man's power.

Mizpah (mĭz′pah) (*watch tower*). A place in Gilead where Jacob made a covenant with Laban, his father-in-law (Gen. 31:49). The words spoken by Laban are frequently quoted today and are known as the Mizpah Benediction.

Moab (mō′ăb). A land east of the Dead Sea and south of the Tribe of Reuben. The Moabites were descendants of Lot's oldest daughter. Balaam, Balak, and Ruth were Moabites.

Molten Sea. The great brazen laver in the Priests' Court of the Temple. It was supported by twelve brazen bullocks. (See *laver.*)

monotheism (mŏn'o-the-iz-'m). A belief in one God.

Moriah, Mount (mo-ri'ah) (*Jehovah provides*). A hill in Jerusalem, originally used as a threshing floor. It is generally believed to be the place where God sent Abraham to sacrifice Isaac. It became the site of the three temples built by Solomon, Zerubbabel, and Herod.

Nazarite (năz'ă-rīte) (*one separated*). A consecrated Hebrew, set apart from others for the service of God. He was forbidden to use wine, cut his hair, or touch a corpse. Three Nazarites mentioned in the Bible are Samuel, Samson, and John the Baptist.

Nebo (ne'bō). A mountain from which Moses viewed the Promised Land. It is in Moab directly across the Jordan River from Jericho.

Nineveh (nin'e-veh). An ancient city of Assyria founded by Nimrod (Gen. 10:11). The prophet, Jonah, was sent to preach to this great city "of three days' journey."

Numbers. The fourth book of the Pentateuch, so-called because it gives accounts of two numberings of the Hebrews, one taken at Mount Sinai and the other just before the entrance into the Promised Land.

offering (ŏf'er-ing). That which is presented to God through confession, consecration, or thanksgiving.

oracle (ŏr'ă-k'l). A term sometimes applied to the Temple or any holy place where God made his will known to man.

Palestine (păl'es-tīne). See *Promised Land.*

Passover (pas'o'ver). An annual Jewish spring feast commemorating two events: the sparing of the first-born when God smote the Egyptians and their deliverance from Egyptian bondage.

patriarch (pa'tri-ärk) (*father*). One who governs his family or descendants by paternal right. The term is applied to Abraham, Isaac, Jacob, and Joseph.

Pentateuch (pĕn′tȧ-tūk) (*five books*). The Greek name for the first five books of the Old Testament. The Jews call it the Torah.

Pharaoh (fâr′ō). The official title of the Egyptian kings. Eight pharaohs are mentioned in the Bible.

Philistines (fĭ-lĭs′tīnes). The inhabitants of Philistia, a strip of country about forty or fifty miles in length, lying along the Mediterranean coast and bordering Palestine on the southwest. The Philistines were never conquered by the Israelites.

Phoenicia (fē-nĭsh′ĭ-ȧ). A narrow strip of land lying along the Mediterranean coast north of Palestine. It extended east to the Lebanon Mountains. Tyre and Sidon were the two principal cities.

plague (plāg). A scourge, a calamity, or a disease. Of the ten plagues God sent upon the Egyptians, many struck at their objects of worship: the Nile River, frogs, cattle, etc.

polytheism (pŏl′ĭ-thē-ĭz-'m). A belief in many Gods.

post-exilic (pōst′ĕg-zĭl′ĭk). The period following the return of the Hebrews from the Babylonian exile, 536 B.C.

pre-exilic (prē′ĕg-zĭl′ĭk). The period before the Babylonian exile which began in 606 B.C.

prologue (prō′lŏg). The preface or introduction to a poem, speech, or discourse.

Promised Land. A country lying along the east shore of the Mediterranean Sea. Its average length is about 140 miles and its width about 25 to 75 miles, embracing an area of about 12,000 square miles. It was called Canaan, the Holy Land, and Palestine. This land was repeatedly promised to Abraham and his descendants. It is sacred to Christians, Jews, and Mohammedans.

prophet (prŏf′ĕt). See page 49.

prophecy (prŏf′ē-sī), *noun*. The prediction of a prophet. The foretelling of events through divine guidance.

prophesy (prŏf'ĕ-sī), *verb*. To speak with divine inspiration; to foretell.

proverb (prŏv'ûrb). See page 36.

Psalter (sôl'tẽr). The Book of Psalms. See page 35.

Rameses (rȧ-mē'sēz). One of the treasure cities of the Land of Goshen built by the children of Israel during the oppression.

Sabbath (săb'ȧth) (*day of rest*). The seventh day of the week in the Jewish calendar. God worked six days and rested on the seventh, setting it apart for himself. The Jews and some Christians still observe the seventh, but the majority of Christians observe the first day or Sunday as the Sabbath or day of rest.

Samaria (sȧ-mā'rĭ-ȧ). A city of Ephraim and capital of the Ten Tribes of Israel. Ahab built a temple to the heathen god, Baal, in Samaria.

scorpions (skôr'pĭ-ŭns). Whips having several lashes with leaded balls attached and hooks projecting from them.

Septuagint (sĕp'tu-ȧ-jĭnt) (*seventy*). See page 66.

Shechem (shē'kĕm). An important ancient city of Palestine, lying between the two mountains, Gerizim on the south and Ebal on the north. When Abraham entered the Promised Land, he pitched his tent at Shechem and built an altar. Jacob purchased land here and dug his famous well. Joshua gathered all Israel here and delivered to them his farewell message. It was one of the capital cities of the Northern Kingdom.

shewbread (shō'brĕd). Unleavened bread to be eaten only by the priests. It was prepared anew and placed every Sabbath upon the ten tables in the Temple. On each table were twelve loaves representing the twelve tribes.

Sinai (sī'nī). The mountain from which God gave the Law to Moses. It is in the center of the peninsula formed by the two horns of the Red Sea. It is also called Mount Horeb.

Syria (sĭr′ĭ-à). A land north of Palestine bordered on the west by Phoenicia and on the northeast by the Euphrates River and on the southeast by the Arabian Desert. The chief city was Damascus.

Tabernacle (tăb′ûr-năk′'l). A tent of worship constructed by Moses and the Israelites under divine direction. It was built before the close of the encampment at the foot of Mount Sinai and was carried by the Israelites in their wanderings. Over it hovered the pillar of cloud by day and the pillar of fire by night.

Testament (tĕs′tà-mĕnt). See *covenant.*

Tigris (tī′grĭs). A river which rises in the Armenian mountains and flows into the Euphrates River. In the Garden of Eden it is called Hiddekel.

Tithe (tīth) (*tenth part*). A form of taxation practised by the Hebrews who were required to give to the service of the Lord one tenth or a tithe of their income. The custom still survives among many Christians.

Torah (tō′rä). The Hebrew name for Pentateuch, or Law of Moses.

Tyre (tīre). An ancient Phoenician city on the Mediterranean coast. Hiram, King of Tyre, was a friend of David. He assisted Solomon in the building of the Temple supplying cedar and workmen.

Ur (ûr). The place where Abraham and his family were living when God called him to go into the Promised Land. It was probably on the Euphrates River near the head of the Persian Gulf.

veil (vāl). A curtain of "blue, and purple, and crimson, and fine linen" which hung in the Temple before the Most Holy Place. When Christ died on the cross, this veil was "rent in twain from top to bottom." (Matt. 27:51.)

vow (vou). A solemn promise made to God.

Price List

WallBuilders, Inc.
P.O. Box 397
Aledo, TX 76008
(817) 441-6044

Prices subject to change without notice
Quantity and case-lot discounts available

Books

America: To Pray or Not To Pray?
A statistical look at what has happened when religious principles were separated from public affairs by the Supreme Court in 1962.

The Myth of Separation
An examination of the writings of the Framers of the Constitution and of the Supreme Court's own records concerning the proper role of religious principles in society.

The Bulletproof George Washington
An account of God's miraculous protection of Washington in the French and Indian War and of Washington's open gratitude for God's Divine intervention.

The New England Primer
A reprint of the 1777 textbook used by the Founding Fathers. It was the first textbook printed in America (1690) and was used for 200 years to teach reading and Bible lessons in school.

Noah Webster's "Advice to the Young"
Founder Noah Webster stated that this work "will be useful in enlightening the minds of youth in religious and moral principles and serve to restrain some of the common vices of our country." These timeless lessons are still invaluable for today's youth.

Bible Study Course—New Testament
A reprint of the 1946 New Testament survey text used by the Dallas Public High Schools.

Bible Study Course—Old Testament
A reprint of the 1954 Old Testament survey text used by the Dallas Public High Schools.

What Happened in Education?
Statistical evidence that disproves several popular educational explanations for the decline in SAT scores.

Did Television Cause the Changes in Youth Morality?
This exam is very enlightening not only as to what happened in television, but when it happened, and why?

"Great Americans" Poster Series
Because of the growing interest in restoring our true history and documenting the lives and philosophies of prominent Americans, WallBuilders offers a series of posters designed to give an enjoyable overview of great men and women in America's history (George Washington, Pocahontas, Abraham Lincoln, George Washington Carver, and Thomas Jefferson). These beautiful 16 x 20 informational posters are excellent for use in public, Christian, or home schools.

Pamphlets

The Truth About Thomas Jefferson and the First Amendment
For the past three decades, Thomas Jefferson has often been pointed to as *the* authority on the First Amendment, yet for 170 years prior, he was rarely cited in conjunction with that Amendment. This pamphlet explains the common misconception concerning Jefferson's role with the First Amendment and turns us to the men who did have an influence on it—men such as George Washington, Gouverneur Morris, and Fisher Ames.

Video Cassette (VHS)

America's Godly Heritage (60 min.)

This clearly sets forth the beliefs of many of the famous Founding Fathers concerning the proper role of Christian principles in education, government, and the public affairs of the nation.

Keys to Good Government (59 min.)

Presents the beliefs of the Founders concerning the proper role of Biblically thinking principles in education government, and public affairs.

Education and the Founding Fathers (60 min.)

A look at the Bible-based educational system which produced America's great heroes. It is excellent for learning what was intended by the Founders for America's schools.

Spirit of the American Revolution (53 min.)

A look at the motivation which caused the Founders to pledge their "lives, fortunes, and sacred honor" to establish our new nation.

Foundations of American Government (25 min.)

Surveys the historical statements and records surrounding the drafting of the First Amendment, showing the Founders's intent.

Video Transcripts

America's Godly Heritage (See video)
Education and the Founding Fathers (See video)
Foundations of American Government (See video)
Keys to Good Government (See video)
Spirit of the American Revolution (See video)

Audio Cassette Tapes

Religion & Morality, Indispensable Supports

This tape documents the statements of many Founding Fathers who agreed with Washington that religion and morality are indispensable supports for American society.

Thinking Biblically, Speaking Secularly

Provides guidelines for Biblically thinking individuals to effectively communicate important truths in today's often anti-Biblical environment.

The Founding Fathers

Highlights accomplishments and notable quotes of prominent Founding Fathers which show their strong belief in Christian principles.

The Laws of the Heavens

An explanation of the eight words in the Declaration of Independence on which the nation was birthed.

America: Lessons from Nehemiah

A look at the Scriptural parallels between the rebuilding of Jerusalem in the book of Nehemiah and that of America today.

8 Principles for Reformation

Eight Biblical guidelines for restoring Christian principles to society and public affairs.

America's Godly Heritage (See video)
Keys to Good Government (See video)
Education and the Founding Fathers (See video)
The Spirit of the American Revolution (See video)
Foundations of American Government (See video)
The Myth of Separation (See book)
America: To Pray or Not To Pray (See book)

Title	Stock#	Price	Quantity	Total
Books/Pamphlets				
America: To Pray or Not to Pray	(B01)	$6.95	_____	_____
The Myth of Separation	(B02)	$7.95	_____	_____
The Bulletproof George Washington	(B05)	$4.95	_____	_____
The New England Primer	(B06)	$5.95	_____	_____
Noah Webster's "Advice to the Young"	(B10)	$4.95	_____	_____
New Testament Bible Study—Dallas H.S.	(B09)	$4.95	_____	_____
Old Testament Bible Study—Dallas H.S.	(B12)	$4.95	_____	_____
What Happened in Education?	(B03)	$2.95	_____	_____
Did TV Cause the Changes in Youth Morality?	(B04)	$2.95	_____	_____
Thomas Jefferson and the First Amendment	(PAM01)	$ .50	_____	_____
Video Cassette (VHS)				
America's Godly Heritage	(V01)	$19.95	_____	_____
Keys to Good Government	(V05)	$19.95	_____	_____
Education and the Founding Fathers	(V02)	$19.95	_____	_____
Spirit of the American Revolution	(V04)	$19.95	_____	_____
Foundations of American Government	(V03)	$ 9.95	_____	_____
Video Transcripts				
America's Godly Heritage	(TSC01)	$2.95	_____	_____
Education and the Founding Fathers	(TSC02)	$2.95	_____	_____
Foundations of American Government	(TSC03)	$2.95	_____	_____
Keys to Good Government	(TSC04)	$2.95	_____	_____
Spirit of the American Revolution	(TSC05)	$2.95	_____	_____
Audio Cassette Tapes				
Religion & Morality, Indispensable Supports	(A14)	$4.95	_____	_____
Thinking Biblically, Speaking Secularly	(A13)	$4.95	_____	_____
The Founding Fathers	(A11)	$4.95	_____	_____
The Laws of the Heavens	(A03)	$4.95	_____	_____
America: Lessons from Nehemiah	(A05)	$4.95	_____	_____
8 Principles for Reformation	(A10)	$4.95	_____	_____
America's Godly Heritage	(A01)	$4.95	_____	_____
Keys to Good Government	(A09)	$4.95	_____	_____
Education and the Founding Fathers	(A08)	$4.95	_____	_____
The Spirit of the American Revolution	(A02)	$4.95	_____	_____
Foundations of American Government	(A12)	$4.95	_____	_____
The Myth of Separation	(A06)	$4.95	_____	_____
America: To Pray or Not to Pray	(A07)	$4.95	_____	_____
Great Americans Poster Series				
Poster Set (5 posters)	(P01)	$19.95	_____	_____
George Washington Carver	(P02)	$ 4.95	_____	_____
Thomas Jefferson	(P03)	$ 4.95	_____	_____
Abraham Lincoln	(P04)	$ 4.95	_____	_____
Pocahontas	(P05)	$ 4.95	_____	_____
George Washington	(P06)	$ 4.95	_____	_____

When shipping products to multiple addresses, please calculate shipping cost based on the dollar amount to each address—not on the order total. Thank you.

Please allow 4-6 Weeks for delivery.

WallBuilders, PO Box 397, Aledo, TX 76008

SubTotal: _____
Tax (TX only, add 7.75%): _____
Shipping (see chart below): _____
TOTAL: _____

Canada orders add $5 extra.

Under $5.00 . . . . $2.00	$25.01-$ 40.00 . . $6.45	
$ 5.01-$15.00 . . $3.45	$40.01-$ 60.00 . . $7.45	
$15.01-$25.00 . . $4.45	$60.01-$140.00 . . $9.95	
	Over $140 7%	